50p

PC Buyer's
Survival Guide

Computer users are not all alike.
Neither are SYBEX books.

We know our customers have a variety of needs. They've told us so. And because we've listened, we've developed several distinct types of books to meet the needs of each of our customers. What are you looking for in computer help?

If you're looking for the basics, try the **ABC's** series, or for a more visual approach, select **Teach Yourself**.

Mastering and **Understanding** titles offer you a step-by-step introduction, plus an in-depth examination of intermediate-level features, to use as you progress.

Our **Up & Running** series is designed for computer-literate consumers who want a no-nonsense overview of new programs. Just 20 basic lessons, and you're on your way.

SYBEX **Encyclopedias** and **Desktop References** provide a comprehensive reference and explanation of all of the commands, features and functions of the subject software.

Sometimes a subject requires a special treatment that our standard series don't provide. So you'll find we have titles like **Advanced Techniques, Handbooks, Tips & Tricks**, and others that are specifically tailored to satisfy a unique need.

You'll find SYBEX publishes a variety of books on every popular software package. Looking for computer help? Help Yourself to SYBEX.

For a complete catalog of our publications:

SYBEX Inc.
2021 Challenger Drive, Alameda, CA 94501
Tel: (510) 523-8233/(800) 227-2346 Telex: 336311
Fax: (510) 523-2373

PC Buyer's Survival Guide

Harald Babiel

Rainer Babiel

SYBEX®

San Francisco • Paris • Düsseldorf • Soest

Acquisitions Editor: David J. Clark
Translator: Tristan Translations
Editor: Carol Henry
Project Editor: Abby Azrael
Technical Editor: Sheldon Dunn
Word Processors: Ann Dunn and Chris Meredith
Book Designer: Elke Hermanowski
Desktop Production Artist: Charlotte Carter
Production Coordinator: Catherine Mahoney
Indexer: Ted Laux
Cover Designer: Ingalls+Associates
Cover Illustrator: Harumé Kubo

Contents

Foreword

386SX-20

20 MHz, O wait states, 2Mb RAM on board, up to 8Mb

256K, 16-bit VGA card

1.2 Mb and 1.44Mb drives

40Mb, 28 ms IDE hard disk

1 serial. 1 parallel port

Extended keyboard

14" VGA color monitor

1024 × 68, .28 dot pitch

$999

Did you get all that?

The list above is a typical advertisement in a computer magazine. If you cannot judge whether this is a good deal, or you do not know why you need a 1.2Mb disk drive with 2Mb RAM, you made the right move in buying this book.

In the next 20 chapters, we will explain these relationships and help you select your computer workstation. The term *workstation* refers to basic equipment (hardware) and some of the programs (software) with which you will work. You will learn how to make your hardware and software work together to meet your computer needs.

Harald and Rainer Babiel
Haltern, February 1992

Chapter 1

What Is a PC?

There are many different small computers that claim the designation of "personal computer," or PC for short. However, there is only one world standard: the IBM-compatible PC. This one is what this little book is all about.

The Early Years

The first IBM PC appeared over ten years ago. It was not the first computer of its size on the market, and it certainly was not the most powerful. However, IBM was a computer manufacturer with a worldwide reputation and a significant sales and service network. And the design of the PC as an "open" (expandable) system, though derided by many when introduced in 1981, was a major factor contributing to the PC's success.

The IBM consisted of many proven or, from another point of view, obsolete components from various third-party manufacturers. It also had slots for adding other components and accessory features. Because of these slots, you were able to purchase a basic model and expand it over time as your requirements increased. Moreover, you did not need to purchase IBM products to expand the computer's power. You could use the products of other manufacturers.

An "open" system

When the IBM PC became successful, other manufacturers began producing copies of individual components—or even the whole computer. Almost all these copies, or *clones*, incorporated improvements that accelerated the development of PC hardware and the software used thereon. The IBM PC was also a windfall for program developers. A newly developed program needed only to run on the IBM PC to be able to run on all compatible clones. There were soon many programs available for the PC. People therefore bought the PC in spite of its less-than-perfect technical performance (as compared to competing products). This made the IBM PC the standard computer for office applications.

Development

1983:
the XT

IBM offered its PC on the international market at the beginning of 1983. In the same year, IBM equipped the PC for the first time with a hard disk. This model was designated the PC/XT; XT stands for "eXtended Technology." The XT abbreviation is still used today as a collective term for all IBM-compatible computers with an Intel 8088 or 8086 microprocessor—the central component of the PC. Further development of the PC has been closely linked to the development of the microprocessor.

The first IBM model contained an Intel 8088 processor. This processor is a simplified version of the Intel 8086 that became the grandfather of the PC development. All processors used in PC successors (based on Intel 80xxx processors) are compatible with the 8086; this is known as "downward compatibility." It means they understand the same instructions as their grandfather.

1984:
the AT

The "Advanced Technology" model followed the XT model in the autumn of 1984. The corresponding abbreviation, AT, then became the designation for all IBM PCs and their clones containing the then new Intel 80286 processor. Besides running programs faster, one significant new property of this processor was an additional, enhanced operating mode with substantially increased performance.

This time, however, software developers did not quite keep pace. Most programs did not exploit the new enhanced mode. The 80286 processor, therefore, runs in most PCs only as a fast 8086. Only recently have a few programs fully exploited the capabilities of the 80286.

Microprocessor development continued with the 80386 and 80486 models. The full power of these new processors is still not fully used today. In spite of this, computers containing these processors are extremely popular because of their faster operating speed.

Portable Computers

Once the PC had entered virtually every business and most home office environments, the need was recognized for a computer that could be used while traveling. Different designs were tried. Today, the *laptop* and *notebook* models have met with the greatest acceptance.

A laptop weighs up to 22 pounds and can be easily transported because of its compact design. Laptops frequently come with a battery pack, but these last only a few hours because of the machine's substantial power requirements.

Laptops

Notebook computers weigh only about 6.5 pounds. When folded up, they look like an 8•-by-11-inch pad of paper about 2 inches thick. With these computers, you flip up the screen and operate the computer with a conventional keyboard. The screen does not look like a television, but is usually a liquid-crystal display (LCD).

Notebooks

Because of its very compact design, a notebook PC is well suited for travel. It fits in an attaché case. Operation for several hours without connecting to a live power source is possible because of power-saving components in these machines.

Perspectives

Hardware development has been running several lengths ahead of software since the market introduction of 80286 PCs. Only now, years later, is the power of this model being utilized by a program with some market significance: Windows 3.1. And the limits of 32-bit technology introduced in the PC arena by the 80386 processor (see Chapter 3) are still far away.

Consequently, hardware developers probably will turn more to product maintenance in the next years than to developing completely new technologies. The 80486 processor demonstrates this trend. It integrates known components, thereby achieving simpler, more compact design of the PC, while also increasing operating speed.

Although no surprises are expected in the further development of microprocessors, you can look forward to considerable technical advances in other PC components. The hard disk, of course, and even the video and sound capabilities of PCs will improve and increase dramatically. The buzzword, *multimedia*, has been surfacing for some time now in technical journals.

Finally, bear in mind that no matter when you buy your PC, after a few months it will no longer be the latest "state of the art."

Chapter 2

PC Design

*IBM designed the PC as an open system, so that individual compo-
nents can easily be replaced, removed, and added.*

Cases

The original design of the PC's housing was restricted to a very few
implementations. Today, there are several versions for different
purposes.

A tower is an upright unit usually located next to or beneath a desk.
This design makes it more difficult to turn the computer on and off
or to insert a floppy disk, but it saves space on the desktop. Tower
cases are also generously sized, and provide a lot of space for
expansion.

Towers

The most popular case design is the desktop version. It sits on top of
the desk and uses a lot of space, but you can operate it without
twisting and turning. The monitor is usually placed on top of the PC
case, which saves some desktop area.

Desktops

Besides the standard desktop PC case, there are also slim-line and
baby AT cases. Slim-lines have a particularly thin case; baby ATs
have a case with an especially small footprint.

Notebook and laptop designs have gained market share. Both are
portable devices, and the notebook PC can easily be used while
traveling because of its low weight and small size. High component
integration allows this compact size. The disadvantage of these PC
versions is that they usually lose the character of open systems,
which means you cannot easily expand them.

The System Board

The case of a conventional PC contains several components. The important *system board* holds the central microprocessor; this board is also known as the *motherboard*. Besides the microprocessor and additional electronic elements, the system board also holds the main memory components: the RAM (random access memory).

It's important to look on the motherboard for the name of the BIOS (Basic Input/Output System) used by the manufacturer. The BIOS is crucial in determining the extent of your system's IBM-compatibility. The brand name is printed on the chip, and usually is displayed on the monitor when the computer is started.

Today's more advanced motherboards may also have on-board cache memory for accelerating the operation of the microprocessor. The cache memory is not as readily identifiable as the BIOS, and you'll want to ask your computer dealer whether there is cache memory, and how much.

If you are building your own system, you should also be sure that the motherboard is designed to fit into the case that you want. Problems are uncommon, but because of slight differences in motherboards (for example, in the number of expansion slots or location of the keyboard port), you need to verify that the components will fit together.

Main Memory

The amount of main memory helps determine the performance of your PC. Mounting this memory directly on the motherboard provides an additional improvement in performance. For more on this topic, see Chapter 4, Memory.

Slots and Add-in Cards

Add-in cards are exchangeable components that perform some important tasks in a PC. These cards are usually printed circuit boards with soldered or integrated connectors. Sockets for these connectors, mounted on the motherboard, are known as *slots*. A few of these slots are usually occupied by add-in cards when your PC is first assembled. Other slots can hold later component additions. The more open slots a PC provides, the more components you can add. For example, you might add a memory expansion board, a sound card, or a connection to the telephone network.

Add-in cards plug into slots

Video Cards

The screen adapter is one of the cards usually provided as standard equipment in a PC. These add-in cards are also known as *video cards* and, depending upon their operation, may be VGA cards, XGA cards, and the like. The video card controls the display of text and graphics information on the computer's screen, or *monitor*. The card converts the characters to be displayed into information that the screen logic can understand and represent.

Just like a television set, the image on a computer monitor must be continuously updated. The video card does this by remembering the current contents and constantly refreshing the image. The quality of the image that you see depends on both the video card and the monitor, and on an optimal combination of these two components.

Controllers

The floppy drives and the hard drive(s) are controlled in PCs by either two separate *controller cards* or a single combined (multifunction) controller. Either type can handle from one to four floppy drives and up to two hard drives. Some hard drives even come mounted on their controller card, taking up the space of two slots inside the case, but not using a drive bay. The controller handles data exchange between the PC and its disk storage units.

Multifunction controllers

Ports

The *ports* of a PC allow contact with the outside world. Ports are connectors that can be reached from the outside, for attaching peripheral devices. Ports for devices such as the keyboard and mouse are frequently integrated on the motherboard. Each PC will also typically have at least one serial and one parallel port. The parallel port is needed for interfacing with (connecting to) one or more printers, and—more and more these days—with external tape backup units and SCSI hard drives. A serial port lets you connect several additional devices, such as a mouse or a device for data transmission (a modem or a telephone coupler). A major distinction between parallel and serial ports is that a parallel port is limited to connecting a device no more than 20 feet away. Serial devices have been used 650 feet from a PC.

Parallel printer connection, serial mouse

As mentioned, a few PC manufacturers integrate one serial and one parallel port on the motherboard. Others add these ports on the video card; this then becomes a multi-I/O (input/output) card. Still others offer separate add-in port cards. This last variation is the least attractive, because the additional card takes up an available slot.

In advertisements, a PC is frequently described as having "two serial ports, and one parallel"; or "2 x serial, and 1 x parallel." Such a PC has two serial ports and one parallel port.

The Power Supply

All components within the PC case, plus the keyboard and the mouse, if present, get power from a built-in power supply. The power supply also must have enough spare capacity for additional components, such as a tape drive.

Ventilation

The electrical components of a computer generate heat. This means they get hot. To protect them from heat failure, PCs are equipped with fans, which constantly circulate cooling air. The level of operating temperature has a major effect on the life of electronic components. Therefore, complete, adequate ventilation is considered very important in the design of high-grade computers. You can usually assume that even common clone PCs have adequate cooling mechanisms.

The fan in your machine will make some noise and, over time, this may be annoying to you. Choose a system with a fan that is as quiet as possible. In some machines, the temperature is constantly monitored at critical points within the computer. This information is used to control the fan output accordingly or even to sometimes turn it off.

Fans

In Figure 2.1, you can see the power supply with its fan at the top right, hard disk and floppy disk drive at the bottom-right and center respectively, and the speaker at the bottom-left. The motherboard underlies most of the space to the left of center, and perpendicular to the motherboard, you can see some add-in cards and some empty card slots.

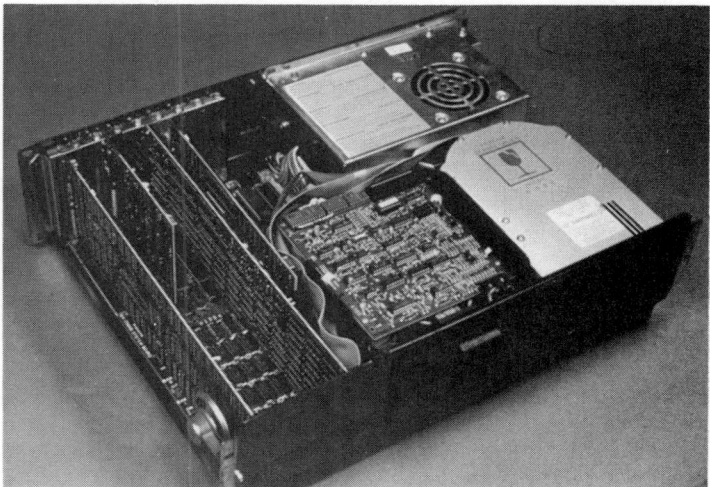

Figure 2.1: Photograph of a PC interior. Photo courtesy of International Business Machines Corporation.

Floppy Disk and Hard Disk Drives

You cannot operate a computer effectively unless you are able to store data permanently. The first PCs used a very slow cassette recorder to store programs and data. Today, almost every PC comes with one or more floppy disk drives and a hard disk. The exceptions are special workstations connected to networks; these computers do not need a drive because they can load programs they need and transmit data over the network.

Half-height drives

Hard drives are available in many sizes: full-size for 5.25-inch disk diameter; half-height for 5.25-inch and 3.5-inch disk diameter; third-height for 3.5-inch disk diameter; and the new "matchbook size." Floppy drives are available in full and half-height for 5.25-inch disks, and in half- and third-height for 3.5-inch disks. Full-sized hard disk drives are now made only for very large storage requirements. The half-height drive has become the common standard for hard drives; for floppy drives, the half- and third-heights are the most common.

A few PCs, for example, the Micro Channel desktop models of IBM, only provide mounting space (drive bays) for 3.5-inch drives. Drive bays for the 5.25-inch format have more flexibility because they can hold either 5.25-inch drives or the smaller 3.5-inch units, using an adapter kit. You will read about the technical differences between the various drive types in Chapters 5 and 6.

BIOS

Configuring components

A common characteristic of all components of a PC is that the central processing unit (CPU) will not directly communicate with them. Communication between the components and the main processor requires the help of a special program known as the Basic Input/Output System, or BIOS for short. Critical information about the type of each component is recorded in a portion of the BIOS known as the *setup*.

The dealer usually performs the BIOS setup, and you need not normally be concerned about this initially. However, you should not completely forget the BIOS. If, for example, you want to add a larger and faster hard disk, you will have to modify the BIOS setup accordingly. You may then get an unpleasant surprise: Your old BIOS may not be capable of recognizing the new hard disk. In this case, check with your computer dealership to find out if there is a newer version of the BIOS, and whether the dealership will load it into your machine.

IBM no longer provides BIOS upgrades for the two 8088 models, PC and XT.

Chapter 3

Processors and Bus Architecture

The central component of every computer—from simple pocket calculator to mainframe—is the microprocessor. The microprocessor is a silicon chip (see Figure 3.1) that integrates the properties of many thousands of transistors and other electronic components. This chip is placed in a plastic housing and connected to the other computer components by means of multiple pins. The number of pins depends on the model of the microprocessor.

Unlike hard-wired circuits, a microprocessor is programmable and thus more flexible. It loads its instructions from a storage device, such as a hard drive, and performs the tasks outlined by the loaded program.

For some special tasks, additional processors, called coprocessors, support the microprocessor. To differentiate it, the central microprocessor is known as the central processing unit (CPU).

Figure 3.1: An Intel microprocessor chip. Photo courtesy of International Business Machines Corporation.

Memory Addressing

The microprocessor loads program commands into the *main memory*. (You'll learn more about memory in Chapter 4.) Think of this main memory as a row of houses with consecutive house numbers. To find the right position in the main memory, the processor must know the address (house number) of the memory location. The address lines of the processor serve this purpose. The number of address lines a microprocessor has is an essential characteristic of the processor.

Using the house number example, suppose you have only two-digit house numbers available. With these, you can address a maximum of 99 houses. If you add a third digit, you can address 999 houses. The situation with processor address lines is similar. The more lines the processor has, the more memory locations it can address. However, because your computer does not calculate in the decimal system, but rather in the binary number system, it needs a lot more digits. With 20 lines, it can address about 1 million locations; with 24 lines, more than 16 million.

The Data Bus

Another important characteristic of microprocessors is the number of lines transmitting the memory contents to the processor. Imagine you want to carry four sacks of potatoes to your cellar. If you are alone, you have to run up and down the stairs four times, making four operations. However, if you have three helpers, the same job is done in one operation, because each of you can take one sack and carry it to the cellar.

Clock cycles

Extend this example to a computer. Rather than four sacks of potatoes, you have a four-digit number, and the term *operation* is now known as a *clock cycle*. If the four-digit number is to be sent to the processor over one line, this requires four clock cycles. However, if four lines are available, the transfer is accomplished in one clock cycle. Because the computer works with binary numbers, you need eight lines to transfer a number that falls between zero and 255 within one clock cycle. Transferring larger values takes more clock cycles and more time.

The first IBM PCs had a microprocessor with eight data lines. More advanced processors have 16 or 32 data lines. These lines are known collectively by the term *data bus*.

The smallest computational unit for a computer is the bit. One line can transfer only one bit, so data buses are typically referred to as 8-bit, 16-bit, or 32-bit.

The System Bus

All the computer's data lines and address lines together, combined with a few other control lines, are referred to as the *system bus*. The term is also used to refer to the specific technical design of the computer. This is known as the computer *architecture*.

There is a distinction between the number of lines of data that the microprocessor can address, and the support of data lines the system bus can pass. The PC and XT models had 16-bit (or 16-line) processors, but the bus (or expansion) slots were only 8-bit slots. Although the AT and newer technology eventually provided 16-bit buses, you can still use an older 8-bit card. The 16-bit expansion slots can be used to insert either an 8-bit card or a 16-bit card.

The AT system bus is wider

The technical design described above has evolved into a worldwide standard, designated as ISA, which stands for Industry Standard Architecture.

Development of the 80386 processor raised similar issues. How could the design of the new system bus accommodate additional lines? For technical and other reasons, IBM broke with the past and developed a completely new system bus, the Micro Channel Architecture, or MCA.

MCA provides substantial technical advantages over the ISA architecture. Unfortunately, however, none of the older expansion cards fit the new system bus. A competing consortium of companies therefore developed what is called the EISA (Extended ISA) architecture. This 32-bit system bus is compatible with the old ISA standard, which means that old add-in cards are still usable. Also,

Older add-in cards still work

the special NEAT connector design allows use of the other lines with special connectors. Therefore, a PC with EISA architecture can be expanded using 8-bit, 16-bit, and 32-bit add-in cards. For reasons of economy, however, most 80386 PCs continue to be configured for the slower (16-bit) ISA bus.

Clock Frequency or Speed

The number of address lines specifies how much main memory the microprocessor can address. The width of the data bus is an important determinant of operating speed, as is *clock speed.*

Millions of clock cycles

Clock speed is measured in clock cycles per second, or *clock frequency.* The unit Hertz, abbreviated Hz, is the common term for this measurement in physics. Because a computer runs at several million clock cycles per second, the abbreviation M, for mega, is appended, to make the term megahertz (MHz). For example, 4 MHz means that the computer executes 4 million clock cycles per second. This does not mean, however, that it also executes 4 million program instructions per second. Many instructions require several clock cycles for execution. PCs currently available on the market have clock frequencies ranging all the way from 4 to 50 MHz.

Wait States

If an add-in card or main memory module operates more slowly than the CPU, the processor must wait for these components. The clock cycles that occur while the CPU is waiting are known as *wait states.* If the PC is equipped with memory that can keep up with the CPU, no wait states are required. This ideal case is frequently abbreviated in advertisements as "0 wait states."

Coprocessors

As mentioned earlier, additional processors, or *coprocessors*, support the CPU in performing special tasks. Some are installed in a PC when it is assembled, and others may be added later. Math coprocessors are particularly important. They supplement the CPU in computations for programs that can detect and use a coprocessor.

A math coprocessor must be matched to the CPU. You can recognize the matching coprocessor type because its type number will be one number higher than that of the CPU. The clock frequency should also match. For example, a 33-MHz 80386 processor needs an 80387 coprocessor of similar speed.

Types of Processors

IBM has set and continues to control standards in the PC world. Since the original IBM PC used Intel processors almost all IBM-compatible clones have also used such processors. Manufacturers such as AMD and Chips & Technologies, provide interesting variations, for example, Chips & Technologies's performance-enhancing NEAT processors. You will probably only notice a price difference in your computer purchase if the motherboard does not use an Intel chip. Since designations of other manufacturers' chips generally refer to the names of Intel models, the following list of the original chips will suffice for most processors.

Successful products are copied

8086

This is the ancestor of PC microprocessors, available since 1978. It has the following characteristics:

16-bit processor

16-bit data bus

20-bit address bus

4.77 to 10 MHz

Note: An *address bus* controls how much RAM memory can be addressed. A 20-bit address is 1Mb; a 24-bit address is 16Mb.

8088

The 8088 is a downsized variant of the 8086 and is the typical XT processor. The difference is in the data bus: 8-bit as opposed to the 16-bit bus in the 8086. The difference between the 8086 and 8088 is similar to the difference between the 32-bit 80386DX and the 16-bit 80386SX. Here are the 8088's capabilities:

16-bit processor

8-bit data bus

20-bit address bus

4.77 to 10 MHz

80286

The 80286, often abbreviated to 286, was installed in the IBM AT computer in 1984. It can address 16Mb via an address bus wider than that of the 8088 processor. Two modes of operation are available: *real mode*, if the machine is running as a faster 8086, and a *protected mode*, with improved memory management and multitasking facilities. The enhanced mode is only available when operating under Windows or OS/2; it is not available under PC-DOS or MS-DOS. The 80286 has these capabilities:

16-bit processor

16-bit data bus

24-bit address bus

8 to 12 MHz

80386

This processor has several current designations, all of which refer to the same primary design: 80386 (often abbreviated to 386), 80386DX, and i386 (the Intel 80386). It has been available since 1986 and first appeared in a COMPAQ PC. This is a 32-bit processor; 16-bit and 32-bit programs may execute in parallel. In *386 enhanced mode,* several applications run from the DOS prompt can be active at one time, under supporting operating systems such as Windows. For other 80386 features in addition to the following characteristics, see the description of the 80286.

32-bit processor

32-bit data bus

32-bit address bus

16 to 25 MHz

80386SX

Introduced in 1988, the 80386SX is a degraded version of the 80386. Internally, it is a 32-bit processor; however, it is limited to the external characteristics of the 80286. This way, it can run programs like its big brother, the 386DX, but can be supported by the more economical peripherals of the 80286. The 386SX is generally slower than an 80286 with the same clock rate. Here are the 386SX's characteristics:

32-bit processor

16-bit data bus

24-bit address bus

16 to 33 MHz

80486

The 80486 has several current model names: 80486 (or 486), 80486DX, and i486. In this chip are integrated the 80386DX, a matching math coprocessor, and a fast temporary memory (cache). Processing of many 80386 commands was also optimized at the hardware level. Here are the 486's characteristics:

Integration

32-bit processor

32-bit data bus

32-bit address bus

25 to 50 MHz

Integrated math coprocessor

Integrated processor cache

80486SX

Though the i486 CPU integrates a math coprocessor, this coprocessor was "crippled" in the 486SX. Cynics have maintained that the 486SX is a defective 486DX. A math coprocessor may be added, but this essentially bypasses the SX processor and you are left with simply the performance of a standard 486DX. The 80486 also integrates a processor cache, which is a portion of reserved memory to hold some of the system program code. The 486SX has these characteristics:

32-bit processor

32-bit data bus

32-bit address bus

20 to 25 MHz

Choosing a Processor

The microprocessor is the central component of your computer and determines its essential characteristics. It is also a major factor in determining the computer's purchase price—not only because of the processor's cost, but also because other components of the computer must be compatible.

The top and bottom ranges of performance are easy to see. An 8088 or 8086 is found in XT computers. This obsolete but inexpensive technology is only suitable for relatively simple applications, such as basic word processing at home.

The i486 processor defines (currently) the highest level. This more-expensive technology provides maximum performance and is usually only required for network servers and CAD (Computer-Aided Design) workstations. If you do not currently have such power requirements but cannot rule out that you may have them in the near future, buy a computer with an 80386 processor and a socket for a math coprocessor. In this way, you can retrofit the machine to closely approximate the performance of an 80486.

The 80286 and 80386SX processors constitute today's midrange. Prices of computers having these two processors with the same clock frequency scarcely differ. With the 80386SX, however, the world of 32-bit programs, such as OS/2 and Windows in 386 enhanced mode, becomes available. In this price range, therefore, the 386SX processor is the better choice.

When selecting the right PC, it is very important to seriously consider the role of your computer, both initially and in the longer term. "The more you have, the more you want" also applies to PCs. It is better to buy a high-performance, bare-bones system that has upgrade potential, than a fully loaded, less-powerful computer.

Chapter 4

Memory

The term memory may refer to two different types of memory. Distinction is usually made between RAM (random access memory), which is temporary and accomplished via memory chips, and permanent storage on devices such as floppy disks.

This chapter covers various forms of chip memory, such as RAM and ROM (read-only memory). Chapters 5 and 6 cover floppy disks, hard disks, and other media.

Main Memory

RAM, which stands for *random access memory*, describes the available main memory in all versions of the PC. With tape storage, the entire tape must be run in order to read information at the end of the tape. With RAM, any position within the RAM can be read or written to directly—thus the designation random access.

Every program instruction and every piece of data must be in main memory before the microprocessor can work with it. Normally, both the entire program and the data used are in main memory.

The capacity of main memory, also known as working memory, is given in kilobytes (K). As already described in Chapter 3, the various microprocessors can address different amounts of memory. These amounts tell you the upper limit of memory that can be used effectively.

Another memory limit was set by Microsoft, developers of the most popular operating system, MS-DOS. The first PC used the 8088 microprocessor; with its 20 address lines, the 8088 can manage a maximum 1 megabyte (Mb) of main memory. However, the developers limited the amount of main memory available for programs to 640K; the remaining 384K is reserved for internal system functions such as video memory.

640K for DOS

Furthermore, the driver programs for expansion hardware were also restricted to the first 640K segment of MS-DOS memory. (*Drivers* are special programs allowing communication among the components of a PC.) These driver programs consume their own share of the amount of main memory available for application programs. As application programs grew in size, less and less main memory was available for data and other uses. Various solutions to this problem have been explored, as described in the following paragraphs.

Expanded Memory

EMS is
LIM

The 384K above the MS-DOS limit are usually not fully utilized. A consortium of applications developers therefore worked out a method to allow MS-DOS programs to access the unused memory. To do this, an executive routine overlays sections of these memory locations into the lower MS-DOS memory. This method is known as the Expanded Memory Specification, or EMS for short. Frequently, it is also known as the LIM standard (the initials of the companies involved: Lotus, Intel, and Microsoft).

Extended Memory

More advanced processors, starting with the 80286, have more address lines. The 80286 and 80386SX can each manage 16 megabytes, and the 80386 and 80486 can each handle up to 4 gigabytes.

XMS

The memory extending beyond 1Mb is designated using the Extended Memory Specification, or XMS. Processors may address this memory directly. However, the limits set by MS-DOS remain. A few application programs contain special functions allowing access to this memory. For example, the Windows graphical user interface replaces many MS-DOS functions, to enable use of this additional memory.

Memory Chips

A PC needs large amounts of main memory. For this reason, it usually comes equipped with inexpensive dynamic RAM chips (also known as DRAM). A SIMM (Single Inline Memory Module) chip has an edge connector with contacts on both sides. A SIPP (Single Inline Pin Package) chip has a single line of pins that are inserted in sockets in the motherboard or memory board. Depending upon the design of the sockets for RAM, either DRAM or SIMMS or SIPPS are used. All RAM chips are not the same. They are available in sizes as small as 8K for older machines, and ranging from 256K up to 4Mb.

In addition to deciding on the kind of RAM chips to use, you must consider the speed of the chips. The speed is measured in nanoseconds (ns), or millionths of a second. Older PCs and XTs with a clock speed of 4.77 MHz used RAM chips with a speed of 150 and 120 nanoseconds (150 is the slower speed). Optimally, speed is matched to the clock speed of the system. A 25-MHz system benefits best from 70ns chips, and a 16-MHz system is best served with a set of 80ns chips. At some point, the speed of a faster RAM chip is of no additional advantage to the processor: Remember—faster is more expensive.

If the computer's power supply is interrupted, RAM chips "forget," because their contents must be refreshed at short intervals. So if there is a power failure or you switch off the PC, it loses all information that was not stored on a floppy disk or hard disk. RAM is therefore used only as working memory or temporary storage.

Short-term memory

When sufficient RAM is available, a *RAM disk* is frequently set up. A RAM disk behaves like a hard disk but is much faster. However, if the power supply is interrupted, a RAM disk, too, loses its contents. This type of storage is suitable primarily for temporary files.

Information that must permanently be kept in the computer, such as the BIOS, cannot be stored in RAM. This information requires static forms of memory, such as ROM, described next.

ROM

ROM is an abbreviation for *read-only memory*. As the name implies, information can only be read from, not written to, these chips.

ROM typically contains the program code. The operating system is stored in ROM and loaded when the computer is first started. The operating system provides the hardware with instructions for the interfacing of all the components—such as using the disk drive to read or write a file, or how to pass data to a printer through the parallel printer port.

In addition to such elementary functions, other programs may be stored in ROM. Older IBM PCs had a BASIC interpreter stored in ROM. This interpreter started automatically when an operating system could not be loaded (for example, because of a defective hard disk). Such built-in programs have the disadvantage that they cannot be easily replaced with new versions.

ROM as static memory retains stored information even after you switch off the computer. If you buy a complete, operational PC, you normally need not concern yourself with ROM and its contents. If you build your computer yourself, you should make sure that the components you use are supported by the system functions burned into the ROM.

Memory Caches

*Fast
temporary
memory*

Cache (pronounced "cash") memory means hidden memory. This is fast temporary memory with two important areas of application. As a disk cache, it speeds up access to the hard disk. As a processor cache, for example, in an 80486 microprocessor, it speeds up the execution instructions.

Instead of using chips (hardware), a disk cache is often emulated today using a program. To do this, some of the RAM is used as temporary memory when a program is either reading from or writing to the disk.

Using cache memory typically results in a considerable acceleration in your PC's performance. Setting up a RAM cache using the driver program supplied, for example, in MS-DOS 5, is effective and not costly.

Purchasing More Memory

Because memory chips have become so inexpensive in recent years, program developers have become greedy about using that memory. Every new version of a program seems to grow exorbitantly, requiring megabytes of disk space and large amounts of main memory. Moreover, setting up a RAM cache or RAM disk, both of which speed up your work with the PC, only makes sense when there is sufficient RAM. There is therefore only one rule to follow when you add memory: The more main memory, the better.

As already mentioned, a PC with an 8088 or 8086 processor can manage a maximum of 1Mb. The effective lower limit is the 640K previously discussed. This is the minimum a new PC should have. When you buy your computer, make sure there are sockets on the motherboard for an expansion to 1Mb; otherwise, adding memory later becomes relatively expensive. The situation is different for computers having at least an 80286 microprocessor. For a PC AT, 640K is no longer state of the art; these computers should have at least 1Mb.

The real test is, however, the software to be used. The program manufacturer gives the minimum requirements for that specific program. Below this limit, the program won't work. At the limit, a program usually limps along. For satisfactory operation, considerably more memory is almost always necessary. Determining the actual amount requires some experience with the particular program. For this reason, check with your dealer, consult technical computer journals, or ask an experienced user.

In almost every PC, main memory can be expanded. Many PC motherboard manufacturers have equipped their products with special sockets and sell matching expansion chips. As an alternative, a PC can also accept a memory expansion board in one of the AT bus slots.

Adding memory later

Expanding the memory on the motherboard is usually considerably less expensive than buying an expansion board. These memory chips also run faster. For this reason, your computer should be able to accommodate as much memory as possible on the motherboard if you plan to expand later. Look for statements such as "2Mb RAM on board, expandable to 8Mb" in the information about your hardware. Here, "on board" means that the working memory on the motherboard of the computer can be expanded to 8Mb.

Chapter 5

Floppy Disks

As explained in Chapter 4, permanent storage of data may be accomplished on several types of media. This chapter discusses floppy disks, typically used for recording and transferring data and programs.

Floppy Disk Construction

A floppy disk is a circular piece of plastic material covered with a thin, magnetic coating. For protection against damage and dirt, the disk is placed in either a flexible or rigid plastic sleeve.

Data is recorded on a floppy disk in the same way that data is recorded on a tape; that is, the surface of the floppy disk is magnetized. Virtually every PC has at least one floppy disk drive into which you insert the floppy disk. This drive rotates the floppy disk, and a read/write head floating closely above the disk surface causes magnetization. An arm moves the read/write head over the disk. The comparison to a record player is obvious; however, data on a floppy disk is not stored in a single, spiral groove as it is on a record, but rather in concentric circles. Depending upon the disk drive, you can sometimes clearly hear the positioning of the read/write head.

Disk Sizes

Two floppy disk sizes are popular now. The older and cheaper size is the 5.25-inch floppy disk. It is contained in a square, flexible, and usually black plastic sleeve about 5.25 inches square. The newer 3.5-inch floppy disk (Figure 5.1) is becoming more and more popular. This disk is protected by a rigid plastic sleeve and measures about 3.5 by 3.75 inches.

Formatting

Before you can use most floppy disks, you must format them, although today, preformatted disks are commonly available. During

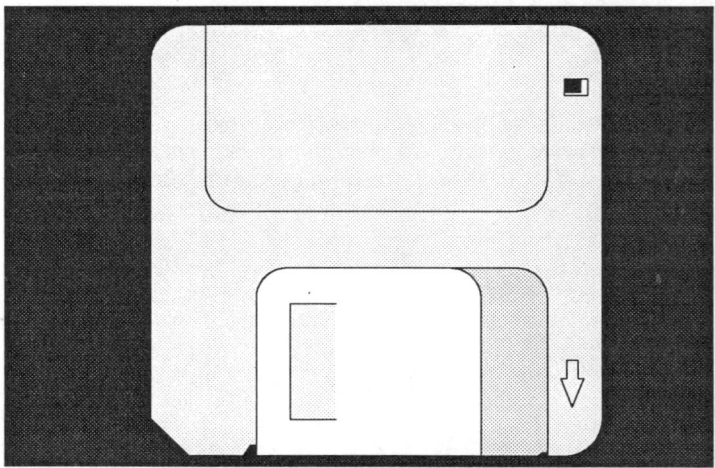

Figure 5.1: A 3.5-inch floppy disk

formatting, the tracks and sectors of the disk are written to a section called the file allocation table (FAT) by the Format program. Also, the magnetization of the floppy disk is checked. Unusable areas are marked as such, bypassed, and reported to you on screen when the formatting is complete.

Storage Capacities

There is more than one method for managing data on a floppy disk. Depending on the method chosen and the composition of the disk surface, two types are popular: double density and high density. As does almost everything else in the PC world, these storage standards come from IBM.

Floppy disks marked "DD" are formatted with *double density*. The 5.25-inch disks then have a storage capacity of 360K; 3.5-inch disks have a capacity of 720K.

The "HD" label on a disk stands for *high density*. After formatting, a 5.25-inch floppy disk has a capacity of 1.2Mb; a 3.5-inch disk has 1.44Mb.

IBM now offers a floppy disk drive for 3.5-inch disks having a capacity of 2.88Mb; such drives are likely to be part of a PC's standard equipment in the near future.

Disk Drives

Floppy disk drives are built to accommodate the various dimensions and recording densities of floppy disks. Drives with high recording densities are designed so that they also work with floppy disks having lower recording densities. A high-density, 5.25-inch disk drive can read and write both 360K and 1.2Mb floppy disks. And 3.5-inch, high-density drives operate similarly. This does not work in the other direction, however. A drive designed only for double-density floppy disks cannot read high-density disks.

Common Abbreviations

Certain abbreviations are typically used to differentiate the various floppy disk types. In addition to the density terms explained just above, you may also see the abbreviation "DS" on the disks. This stands for double-sided. Here are the abbreviations you will see describing the four most common disk formats:

5.25", 360K, DS, DD

5.25", 1.2Mb, DS, HD

3.5", 720K, DS, DD

3.5", 1.44Mb, DS, HD

Deciding What to Buy

The 3.5-inch floppy disks are smaller and hardier. They have a higher storage capacity than 5.25-inch floppy disks.

If your computer will have only a single drive, you should select a 3.5-inch drive with 1.44Mb capacity, rather than 720K.

The principal use of the newer 2.88Mb disk drive is for backing up a hard disk. This is not likely to change until there are more people with whom you can exchange floppy disks in this format. These disk drives are still very expensive.

If the computer you purchased has a 5.25-inch drive, you will not have any problem finding software on this type of floppy disk. In a computer with an 80286 or higher processor, the drive should handle 1.2Mb floppy disks.

It is easiest to work with a computer having both a 3.5-inch, high-density drive and a 5.25-inch, high-density drive.

There are differences between the 3.5-inch drives of various manu-facturers, even in the technical design. In a few drives, the mechanism for ejecting the floppy disks is poorly designed, and you can hurt your finger or break a fingernail. Watch out when you have to push hard to operate the mechanism, or if the drive door has been bevelled by the designer to be "fashionable." (The first IBM PS/2 Model 50 computer provided a glaring example. In this machine, a small push button with a long travel and requiring some force to be pushed was placed in a bevelled recess in the case. Newer IBM PCs no longer have this problem.) Before you buy, try inserting and ejecting a floppy disk. When you open the floppy disk drive, the disk should come out just far enough for you to remove it easily. Avoid buying a disk drive if you have to fish out the disk.

Try to determine how loud the drive is. Some drives make enough noise to wake the dead, particularly when formatting a floppy disk.

Chapter 6

Hard Disks and Other Media

Hard disks can hold large quantities of data. Almost no application program sold today fits on a single floppy disk; many come on a half dozen or more. These programs cannot be started from a floppy disk drive; they must be installed on a hard disk. To accommodate larger individual applications and larger quantities of data moved, hard disks are very important to the effectiveness of a PC workplace.

Hard Disk Structure

The structure of a hard disk is analogous to a stack of floppy disks. Every hard disk consists of one or more coated platters. The coating can be magnetized, just as on a floppy disk, and is used for storing data. Reading and writing of data are accomplished by a set of heads mounted on moving arms that float on a cushion of air above the platters. Even the smallest dust particle can cause large-scale destruction because of the microscopic space between the disk and the heads and the high-speed rotation of the disk, which moves at about 3600 revolutions per minute (rpm). For this reason, the hard disk itself is installed in a sealed, airtight case.

The Controller

The mechanical components that operate the hard disk are inside the sealed drive unit. The electronic circuitry that controls the mechanism is mounted on a board that is external to the drive unit.

One electronic component, the *controller*, handles communication between the hard disk and the CPU. Though hard disks and controllers are available using different technologies, when paired, their technology must match. For this reason, they are discussed here as a single unit.

Speed

As a user, you probably do not care what technology is used—as long as the hard disk provides sufficient storage space and you can access the data quickly. However, the effective speed of a hard disk is related to the technology used.

Average access time

Two quantities are important in this respect.

- *Average access time* is specified in almost every advertisement. This tells you how long it takes, on average, for the read/write heads to find the desired data on the hard disk and transfer this data to the processor. This time is specified in milliseconds (ms).

- The speed of actual transmission of data to the processor is known as the *data transfer rate*. This is specified in megabits per second.

Because the average access time includes the data transfer rate, you may interpret the average access time alone as a measure of the speed of a hard disk.

Interleave Factor

Advertisements for hard disks use the term *interleave factor* more and more. To understand the meaning of interleave, let's look at how hard disk data is accessed.

When a hard disk is formatted, it is prepared to store data. Data is stored in concentric circles (tracks). Each circle is subdivided into individual areas known as *sectors*. While the disk rotates beneath the read/write head, one sector at a time is read and the data is stored in a buffer. Following this, the data can be transferred to the CPU.

This transmission takes time, but the disk continues to rotate. Once the data from one sector has been read from the buffer, the read/write head may have already passed the next sector. The following sector can now be read, but the missed sector cannot be read until the disk completes a rotation.

The interleave factor specifies how many rotations are needed to completely read one disk track. In the example just given, the interleave factor would be 1:2.

Modern hard disks frequently have enough buffer memory to temporarily store one complete data track. In this way, all consecutive sectors of one track can be read during a single rotation of the disk. This optimal behavior is specified as having an interleave factor of 1:1, and achieves the maximum data transfer rate.

In the Beginning: ST506

ST506 was the very first standard for PC hard disks. In this standard, the controller is located in one of the PC expansion slots, and controls up to two hard disks. Two different methods are used to record data: MFM (modified frequency modulation) and RLL (run length limited). In the RLL method, the hard disk is manufactured with closer tolerances than MFM, but is otherwise the same size. RLL achieves a 50 percent greater storage capacity and data transfer rate than MFM. (The data transfer rates are fixed. They do not differ among hard disks using the same recording method.)

ESDI Is Faster

The development of ESDI (Enhanced Small Device Interface) hard disks eliminated some of the restrictions of the ST506 standard. With ESDI, both the data transfer rate and the maximum disk size increased significantly. These disks are still quite popular, but are relatively expensive and are outpaced by current technology.

SCSI, the Universal Genius

The term SCSI (Small Computer Systems Interface), pronounced "scuzzy," defines an interface that can be used to connect up to eight different devices to a computer. These devices include hard disks, printers, and tape drives. In the case of hard disks, the controller is mounted on the disk. In this way, newer recording methods offering higher capacities and greater data transfer rates may be used. The *host adapter* provides the connection to the computer.

SCSI on PC-compatible systems has not reached the same level of popularity as it has on Macintosh computers.

The Hot Topic: IDE

IDE stands for Integrated Drive Electronics. This signifies that the controller logic is integrated into the hard disk. As is the case for SCSI disks, special recording methods having high data transfer rates are possible with IDE. The disk is connected to the computer by means of a conventional expansion slot, and is very inexpensive.

Hard Disks and the CPU

As explained in Chapter 2, the setup procedure of the BIOS tells the processor how many and which hard drives and floppy drives are connected. Let the dealer do this when you purchase your PC. If you wish to replace or add a hard disk, however, you must take care that you have an appropriate disk controller. For example, an IDE disk needs a controller different from that used by an MFM disk.

Specifying the hard disk in the setup

You must also ensure that the hard disk you wish to buy is present in the setup list of the BIOS for your computer. You can read how this is done in the manual that came with your computer.

Other Types of Media

In addition to floppy and hard disks, you can use magnetic tape units (MTU), optical storage devices, and RAM memory to store your programs and data. Tape units have come in several configurations over the past ten years; the most common units today are those that support QIC-40 format and Digital Analog Tape (DAT) units. Optical storage devices may be compact disks with read-only memory (CD-ROMs), WORMs (write-once-read-many), and other forms of optical units. Aside from that for CD-ROMs, an industry standard has not yet been set. The types of RAM memory banks used are nonvolatile memory and a new technology known as Flashcards.

Deciding What to Buy

Hard disks that follow the old ST506 standard are very slow and will also slow down the graphical user interfaces customary in today's software. If you are buying a PC with an 8088 or 8086 processor and do not have high performance requirements, you may choose this type of disk without a second thought. The disk should operate on the RLL method because of the advantages given above. As the data transfer rates have been standardized, the essential selection criterion is now the smallest possible average access time.

ESDI disks were once hot sellers and are still quite popular. However, since there are better alternatives now, you should only buy this type of disk to retrofit an existing computer and controller.

The special properties of the SCSI interface make it the model of choice in network servers because of speed and higher disk capacity.

Single-user computers should be equipped with an IDE disk. This disk combines high speed and advanced drive technology at a reasonable price. IDE controllers are available only for 16-bit machines, 80286 or higher.

Use an
IDE disk

Pay attention to a low average access time. Access times greater than 30 ms are no longer attractive.

In general, observe the following rule when purchasing your equipment: The controller and the hard disk must match. For example, you cannot attach an IDE disk to an MFM controller.

The best size for your hard disk depends on your software and the type of work you want to do on your PC. The size should never be less than 40Mb. You will have sufficient space for normal office applications at 60Mb. Programs that use graphic user interfaces often make 80 to 120Mb a reasonable requirement. For database work with large amounts of data and for programmers, 100 Mb or more may be necessary. Machines in the 80 to 120Mb range are becoming more affordable.

Chapter 7

Video Systems

The words "...incl. monitor and video card..." with cryptic numbers such as "1024 × 768" are often all that you read in advertisements about the most important point of contact between you and the PC you buy. These terms describe the video system—the most important factor of your enjoyment while working or playing with a PC.

This chapter translates advertised technical specifications for video output. It also explains the most important industry standards. You'll read some recommendations for PC equipment for specific jobs, so you can select the most suitable monitor for your PC.

Video Operation

A complete description of the technical processes for generating and maintaining an image on a screen is well beyond the scope of this book. However, here are some basics.

Resolution

Images flickering across a screen are made up of many individual dots known as *pixels*, short for *picture elements*. The more dots available to produce the image, the finer the detail you see. This property is known as *resolution*.

Resolution measures how fine the screen representation is. Resolution is usually specified using two numbers, such as 1024 × 768. By multiplying these numbers, you get the total number of dots that can be displayed. The first number gives the maximum number of dots that can be shown horizontally, that is, in one row. The second number is the number of rows that can be shown. So a resolution of 1024 × 768 specifies that a maximum 768,432 dots can be represented in a rectangle. The rectangle consists of 768 rows, each having 1024 adjacent dots.

Video Cards

To generate an image on a monitor, the CPU must first specify what the image should look like. This information is transmitted to the *video card*. The video card temporarily stores this information in its own memory, and then converts this information into video signals to generate the image on screen.

A video card, also known as a *graphics adapter*, is a circuit board equipped with different circuits. In describing these circuits, most advertisements at least specify the amount of temporary storage (the *video memory*). Usually it consists of from 64K to 1Mb RAM.

On its bottom edge, the video card has a connector that can be inserted into an expansion slot in the PC case. At the rear are the connectors (ports) that connect the video card to the monitor or screen.

The video card in a standard PC is not permanently installed, but located in an expansion slot. You can easily remove it and replace it with a different video card.

Types of Video Cards

The information sent to the video card can be sent in one of two forms. In one case, the processor has already calculated all the dots of the image, and all the video card does is convert these dots into video signals understood by the screen or monitor. Such "dumb" video cards are the most common today.

With "intelligent" video cards, the PC does not calculate all the dots of the screen. Instead, the PC specifies the position, size, and appearance of objects and lets the video card calculate the individual dots. For example, an instruction to the video card might tell it to draw a filled circle of diameter *n* in the center of the screen, and make the inside surface of the circle red.

Because an intelligent video card relieves the CPU of work, total throughput can be significantly increased. However, these video cards are still expensive, and only a few software products are employing their capabilities.

Refresh Rate and Line Frequency

The tasks of a video card are not restricted to just converting an image into video signals and sending these signals to the monitor. The images that the monitor displays are not permanent; they disappear after a few fractions of a second. The video card must send the video signals to the monitor repeatedly to *refresh* the image. If the image is not refreshed fast enough, you will see the picture generated, disappear, generated, disappear, and so on—that is, the image *flickers*.

You'll hear mentioned in advertisements and sales talks one of two quantities for refresh frequency. *Line frequency*, or *horizontal deflection (scan) frequency*, is measured in kilohertz (kHz) and specifies how many thousands of lines of pixels can be generated in one second. *Refresh frequency*, more commonly known as the *refresh rate*, is measured in hertz (Hz) and specifies how often every second the complete picture is refreshed.

Screen flicker

Interlaced vs. Noninterlaced

Two techniques may be used to refresh the image. In one, the image is completely reconstructed from top to bottom. This method is known as *noninterlaced*. In the other method, only every second line of the image is refreshed during each pass. This method, known as interlaced, as invented to refresh the entire image, and is apparently faster for images with high resolution at the same line frequency. This method fools the human eye; even at a lower line frequency, the eye no longer perceives flicker in the interlaced mode.

The *interlaced* technique creates a new problem—The time between refreshing two immediately adjacent lines can become long enough so that the eye perceives flicker between the lines. Because of this, the interlaced mode is not a true solution to the problem of flicker.

Flicker-free at 70 Hz and above

Only a sufficiently high refresh rate provides a satisfactory solution to the problem of flicker. You get a flicker-free image only with a refresh rate of at least 70 Hz (noninterlaced). This is especially true for dark characters against a bright background, and for lengthy computer sessions.

Graphics Standards

Graphics standards have evolved rapidly over the brief history of the PC, mainly because the first standards were inadequate. It is simple to replace an existing video card with another. The effect of such a change is immediately visible on the monitor—as long as the computer, video card, and monitor all match.

Although many of these standards are now "old hat," you should be familiar with their names, so that you don't buy one of these old hats by mistake.

Why are these standards so important? The answer lies in the communication between the CPU and the video card. Unfortunately, this communication does not always operate consistently. Graphics standards ensure proper operation during screen output. Only when a standard has become sufficiently prevalent do applications (such as Windows) get the appropriate drivers allowing the program to use the video system at its greatest capability.

CGA/MDA

Old hats

The first PCs were equipped with video cards developed by IBM. CGA and MDA abbreviations, for the official terms Color Graphics Adapter and Monochrome Display Adapter, quickly became familiar. Other companies soon produced video cards that meet the technical specifications of these graphics standards and are easily interchanged with IBM cards. (Incidentally, the technical design of the CGA card was chosen so that you also could connect a television set to the card.)

CGA and MDA are no longer the video standards of choice. Their performance is quite limited, and they do not even have a substantial advantage in terms of price.

Hercules/MGA

After CGA and MDA came Hercules. The Hercules company developed a video card known as a Monochrome Graphics Adapter (MGA). This card had a resolution of 720 × 348 pixels and a character resolution of 9 × 14 dots. With this resolution, the card could display text cleanly as well as provide a previously unachieved resolution for monochrome graphics. For a long time, the technical specifications of this card served as the new standard.

You can still read advertisements for Hercules-compatible video cards. However, even these cards are now out of favor, because, in the meantime, the availability of more advanced video cards and corresponding monitors has increased. The low 50-Hz refresh rate alone disqualifies the Hercules cards for most modern PC work.

EGA

IBM developed the next standard, the Enhanced Graphics Adapter (EGA). EGA video cards have a maximum resolution of 640 × 350 dots, a refresh rate of 60 Hz, and can represent 16 of 64 colors simultaneously. Building on this, other manufacturers developed EGA cards providing resolutions up to 800 × 600 pixels.

Unfortunately, the higher resolutions were not standardized. Typically, higher resolution could be achieved if additional *drivers* were supplied by the video card manufacturers. These drivers are small software programs supplied on floppy disks. They bridged the gap between the processor and the video card for the high-resolution modes.

Again, only one piece of advice is appropriate here: EGA equipment is no longer adequate for newer systems.

Digital versus Analog Signals

*Analog
instead of
digital*

The video cards described above send digital signals to the screen. The EGA cards exhausted the potential of digital signal transmission. Only with analog signals was it possible to represent shades of gray, color shadows, and a more extensive color palette. However, new monitors were needed for this—monitors able to understand analog signals.

MCGA

The first video card to use analog signals was the Multi Color Graphics Array (MCGA). This video card is installed in a few IBM computers in the PS/2 series. MCGA does not have any discernible advantages over more advanced cards; consequently, we advise against purchasing one if it is ever offered to you.

VGA

*The current
standard*

The Video Graphics Array (VGA) is the type of video card most frequently mentioned today in advertisements. Introduced by IBM in 1987, the maximum resolution of this card is 640×480 pixels in graphics mode, and 720×400 pixels in text mode.

In the maximum graphics mode, only 16 colors (from a palette of 262,144 possible shades) can be displayed simultaneously on the screen. Correspondingly more colors can be displayed if the resolution is lower. The refresh rate is 60 Hz in graphics mode and 70 Hz in text mode. VGA even allows the flicker-free display of dark characters on a bright background.

IBM originally designed the VGA card with 256K RAM as video memory. Today it is customary to start with more memory on the video card.

SuperVGA

Video development did not stop here. VGA cards providing even higher performance were built by other companies. Such SuperVGA cards (or SVGA) have a resolution of 1024 × 768 pixels, refresh rates over 70 Hz, and the potential of displaying 256 colors on the screen at once. However, the video card must then have a 1Mb video memory.

Once video card characteristics exceeded the limits set by IBM, no additional standards were developed. The SVGA video card can achieve such high-resolution modes only if appropriate driver software is available. Every dealer will calm your fears and provide you with the appropriate floppy disk. However, the improvements in the Windows 3.0 and 3.1 graphical user interface (GUI) showed that some graphics card manufacturers had difficulties providing appropriate drivers promptly.

Problems do arise with new software because of the lack of standardization in the high-resolution SuperVGA modes. You should always pay attention to the availability of suitable SVGA drivers when making your purchases.

VGA driver

XGA

In 1991, IBM introduced a new video card known as the XGA, for eXtended Graphics Array. The XGA has a maximum resolution of 1024 × 768 dots at a refresh rate exceeding 60 Hz. It can display 256 colors from a palette of more than a million shades. To date, it has not become a significant force in the market. It can be assumed that XGA will not become the new standard, because of the rapid development of intelligent video cards.

8-Bit or 16-Bit Cards

Occasionally, you will see advertisements stating that the video card is a 16-bit card. This means the card uses the full 16-bit bus to pass the video data. As described in Chapter 3, the term *16-bit bus* means that the processor has 16 data lines. With a 16-bit bus, the processor can read or output 16 bits of data in one clock cycle.

As a rule, the 16-bit video card also has 16 data lines. In theory, this card can operate faster than an 8-bit card. However, not all 16-bit cards work with a bus width of 16 bits. Some chips from Tseng Labs, which appear repeatedly in advertisements, offer complete 16-bit operation. In 1991 comparison tests, video cards equipped with Tseng Labs's ET4000 chip repeatedly performed as the fastest dumb video cards.

Intelligent Video Cards

The limits of conventional video cards became clear as GUIs, such as Windows 3.1, and ever-higher screen resolution became popular. The effective speed of the PC drops if the CPU itself must always calculate all the dots of an image and transmit these dots to the video card.

The obvious solution is to install a processor on the video card. The PC then needs only tell this processor how the image is to appear. Laborious calculation of all individual dots is left to the video card processor.

TIGA cards have "brains"

One such intelligent video card is the TIGA card (developed by Texas Instruments), in which processors with separate program and video memories do some work for the PC. Popularity of these cards suffers because much software still does not support them. Depending on the program used, they can provide tremendous speed advantages, particularly in graphics applications and CAD programs.

Meanwhile, other types of video cards, so-called accelerator cards, have appeared on the market. These are video cards containing graphics chips specially designed to work with graphical user interfaces such as Windows. One example of this is the 8514/A from IBM. These cards have not yet become very popular, but they do provide considerable speed advantages in the graphical interface environment. Be sure to get the necessary driver programs for all applications you wish to use.

Deciding What to Buy

Any purchase recommendations for a video card would be incomplete if they did not also refer to the interaction between the card and the appropriate screen or monitor. Today, VGA cards and even SuperVGA cards and their corresponding monitors have become so inexpensive that older graphics standards cannot be recommended at all. Whether to use color or monochrome in a video card is no longer a question: a VGA card can operate both a monochrome and a color screen.

Any VGA card you consider should have a refresh rate of more than 60 Hz in graphics mode. The more advanced GUIs require refresh rates of 70 Hz; otherwise, with heavy use you will experience eyestrain and fatigue.

At least 70 Hz

The high resolution you see in advertisements is often exaggerated. A maximum resolution of 1024 × 768 can only be used with a large (that also means expensive) screen. The customary 14-inch monitor runs best at a resolution of 800 × 600 pixels. Standard VGA resolutions are also satisfactory. However, if you require high resolution, for example, in a graphics workstation, you should also purchase an appropriate monitor.

Chapter 8

Monitors

The previous chapter addressed the first component of the computer's display system: video cards. Here in Chapter 8 you will read descriptions of and criteria for purchasing a corresponding monitor. You will need these criteria, because the number of different monitors on the market today is staggering. Yet information on the monitor is seldom detailed in advertisements.

First, we will decipher the technical jargon. Following this, we will consider ergonomics, because the deciding factor in selecting the right monitor is your health. Nobody wants to finish a computer session with bloodshot eyes and a headache. Finally, we'll make some recommendations for your purchase.

Monitor Types and Terminology

TTL Monitors

TTL monitors are video displays with digital video-signal input. Suitable only for MDA, CGA, MGA, or Hercules video cards, they are no longer state of the art.

RGB Monitors

RGB monitors are color monitors. They got their name from the fact that three electron beams within these monitors are pointed at a phosphorescent screen that reacts to red, green, and blue. This creates the color image. To prevent color bleeding, a shadow mask is placed in front of the phosphorescent screen, and the electron beams are pointed through this mask. The areas between the dots thus stay dark.

Trinitron Monitors

A Trinitron monitor uses only one electron beam, split into three beams. In these monitors, the phosphor is not activated in a dot pattern but rather vertically, in a striped pattern. The mask has slots rather than round holes. Trinitron screens are characterized by a flat surface. Their graphics images have an annoying property: The vertical and horizontal lines have different thicknesses.

VGA Monitors

The name VGA monitor describes a monitor having an analog signal input operating at the line frequency specified by a VGA card. Monochrome VGA monitors use two colors, one light and one dark (usually black and white). In this category, you can find screens with shadow masks, as well as Trinitron monitors.

Dot Pitch

This term is used repeatedly in monitor descriptions. It specifies the spacing between the centers of the holes or slots in the shadow mask. The smaller this spacing, the more dots can be shown on the screen, and the more detail the image will contain. The most common dot pitch measurements today are .25 (optimum), .27 (the best value), and .31 (the least desirable).

Fixed-Frequency and Multifrequency Monitors

Fixed-frequency monitors can operate at only one horizontal frequency, but you can select from several frequencies if you have a *multifrequency monitor.* Multifrequency monitors are also known as *multisync* or *multiscan* monitors. They detect the horizontal frequency used by a video card, and adapt to this frequency, within limits.

A good multifrequency monitor is your best investment for the future. This is because you don't have to change the monitor if you change your video card. Of course, the bandwidth of possible horizontal frequencies for the monitor you choose should match the video card's horizontal frequencies.

Monitor Size

The size of a monitor is specified as the diagonal measurement of the screen, the same as for a television set.

Currently very popular are 14-inch monitors. These are adequate for most applications. If you plan to make heavy use of DTP (desktop publishing), CAD, or graphics programs, however, or if you want a resolution exceeding 800 × 600, you should buy a larger monitor.

14-inch monitors

Monitor Ergonomics

Although there has been much industry discussion about radiation emitted by video displays, users' health is generally given short shrift. This is true even though the relationship between health complaints and a poor-quality or poorly located monitor is well known. For example, headaches resulting from neck tension may be due to a monitor's being positioned too low or high. Eye fatigue is often caused by flickering screens. These problems alone are sufficient reasons to pay close attention to monitor ergonomics.

Emissions

In recent years, reports have come repeatedly from the U.S. and Scandinavia regarding alleged connections between monitor emissions and health problems, particularly for pregnant women and their unborn children. X rays, and electromagnetic and electrostatic fields were discussed in these reports.

Fortunately, X rays, proven the most dangerous, are also the type of radiation that presents no problems in modern monitors. However, slight traces can still be measured just at the surface of the screen.

X rays are banned

In regard to electromagnetic fields, no connection has yet been proven between health issues and working at a video display. Repeatedly, responsible agencies say this type of radiation in monitors is so weak that damage is improbable. On the other hand, it is technically feasible today to suppress much of the electromagnetic field produced by a monitor, and we recommend that you look for one with the lowest possible emissions.

The electrostatic field that builds up on the computer screen attracts negatively charged dust particles. These particles collect on the surface of the screen. Positively charged particles are repulsed away from the screen, most likely toward the user. There have been reports of eye and skin irritation, but again, no clear connection between the electrostatic charge and health problems has yet been established.

The recommendation we gave for electromagnetic suppression applies here, also. Having no electrostatic field is best, even though it cannot be said with certainty whether it will affect your health. The build-up of an electrostatic field can also be eliminated by today's technology, so look for this feature when you shop.

You should not completely discount the aspect of radiation danger. Though occasional sunbathing at the beach does not absolutely increase the risk of skin cancer, staying outside constantly will most certainly do that. In our opinion, the danger of radiation from a monitor is insignificant if you use the PC only occasionally.

Eliminating Reflection

Mirror, mirror...

It is amazing that there are monitors on the market today that could serve as bathroom mirrors. To keep screen reflection from the work area as low as possible, the screen surface of your monitor should have a clear, antiglare coating. If possible, the entire case should not produce pronounced reflections.

Flicker

In Chapter 7 you learned how a slow image-refresh rate causes the screen to flicker. To the human eye, the screen does not appear completely flicker free until the image-refresh rate is about 70 Hz. The more time you spend working with a computer, the more important it is to have a flicker-free display. The work that you do on the PC also plays a role. If you usually work with bright characters on a dark background, a refresh rate greater than 60 Hz should be sufficient. In the more common screen representation of black type on a white background (paper), you definitely need a refresh rate greater than 70 Hz.

A monitor is only as good as the signals it receives from the video card. When making your purchase, make sure that the video card can also produce the required high refresh rate. Remember that the refresh rate of a video card is directly dependent on the mode in which it is operating.

A video card that has a refresh rate of 70 Hz with a resolution of 640 × 480 dots has a lower refresh rate—less than 50 Hz—with a resolution of 1024 × 768 pixels. Therefore, the desired refresh rate must be achieved at the selected resolution. As explained in the previous section, make sure that the refresh rate is achieved in noninterlaced mode.

Be aware that you can destroy the monitor if you connect it to a video card having a higher horizontal frequency than the monitor can handle. The video card and the monitor must be matched to one another.

Contrast, Convergence, and Focusing

All three of these terms, contrast, convergence, and focusing, are used to describe the level of definition and fuzziness in the screen. We will not discuss the technical causes here, but you should be aware of all such problems when you try out a monitor before buying it.

Here are a few guidelines. Pay attention to the edges of the screen; out-of-focus effects often become obvious there. Also, look at individual letters at various points on the screen. If you see colored edges on individual letters, the electron beams are not focused correctly. Another important criterion is the contour definition of individual letters. You can quickly see whether a monitor has sufficient definition by looking at lowercase letters such as *s*, *a*, and *e*.

Look at the edges

Monitor Height

Many complaints about working with a PC are the result of an incorrectly positioned monitor. The top edge of your monitor should be just about eye-level. For many desktop computers, this is not a problem, because the monitor sits on top of the case.

Adjustable monitor base

The situation is different with tower cases. To achieve the correct height, it is usually necessary to purchase a monitor base and a shelf that raises the monitor about five or six inches. The monitor base should be easily adjustable—you should be able to swivel the monitor and tilt it at an angle, upward or downward, without much effort.

Headaches and bloodshot eyes may have causes other than the quality of the monitor. Light from windows and lamps should not shine directly onto the monitor or into your eyes. Also be sure that you have enough room to adjust the arrangement of the monitor, your seat, and your workspace. The distance between your eyes and the keyboard and the screen should be between 18 and 24 inches. Finally, a visit to your eye doctor can't hurt. Though some vision defects are not much of an annoyance in daily life, the same problems may cause headaches if you work in front of the display monitor for lengthy periods of time.

Deciding What to Buy

As stated previously, the video card and monitor form a unit; they must match. This applies not only to the type (a VGA card for a VGA monitor) but also for the technical characteristics. The maximum resolution and the horizontal frequency or refresh rate should be identical.

At least VGA

Recommendations for monitors are similar to those for video cards. Basic equipment today should be at least a VGA monitor with a resolution of 640 × 480, and a refresh rate greater than 60 Hz, in noninterlaced mode. The more time spent in front of your computer, the higher the refresh rate and resolution should be.

For a 14-inch screen, the resolution should be limited to 600 × 480. Higher resolution makes sense only for bigger monitors. These are used for graphics and technical workstations.

Whether you need a color or monochrome monitor really depends upon the applications you use. Color is usually not required for business programs and office applications. On the other hand, graphics applications and games do require a color monitor. Color saturation (fidelity) is also important.

A multifrequency monitor can adapt to many horizontal frequencies, and you can connect it to a video card with a different line frequency. However, a fixed-frequency monitor that is well matched to the corresponding video card not only produces the same results as a multifrequency monitor, it is also considerably more affordable.

If you can see yourself easily in the screen when the monitor is switched off, it has too much glare.

You can learn a lot about monitor quality by displaying dark letters against a light background. The display should not flicker. Pay attention to the lowercase letters *e*, *s*, and *a*. There should not be a colored ring around the individual letters.

Always get a demonstration of the monitor. Take your time when looking. Remember that several hours of work (or play) at an unsuitable monitor can bring on a headache and ruin your day. Remember: Stay alert when buying a monitor!

Chapter 9

Printers

You will need a printer for almost everything you do. Letters and spreadsheets on the screen aren't that useful if you can't print them on paper. You will also need the right printer. In this chapter, we will again explain a few technical terms, describe the most common printer types, discuss printer costs and related expenses, and give you hints about choosing a printer.

DPI, or Resolution

The most important factor in selecting a printer is its *resolution*, which measures print quality in dots per inch (dpi). In sales literature, you will see it specified with one number or two numbers, for instance, 300 dpi or 300 × 300 dpi.

Resolution descriptions always differentiate between horizontal and vertical resolution. A specification of 400 × 200 dpi says that the printer can print 400 dots per inch in the horizontal direction and 200 dots per inch in the vertical direction. If the values for horizontal and vertical resolution are equal, only one value is specified, so 300 dpi means the same as 300 × 300 dpi.

Horizontal and vertical resolution

The print quality you need depends on how you will use your printer. If you only need a printer to print out data for personal use or for printing the results of your programming (the listings), a resolution as low as 300 dpi is certainly adequate. For business letters, it should be at least letter quality (300 to 360 dpi). Graphics or forms call for higher resolution. Because of their cost, 600 dpi printers are used mostly in the high-end business environment, predominantly for forms and graphics.

Typefaces

To change the appearance of text, you must change the *Typeface*. In addition to common enhancement attributes (boldface, italic, underline, and such), you can also change the typeface quality and style, if your printer is able to support these effects.

Print Quality

The quality of computer-printed text is categorized in three terms: LQ (letter quality), NLQ (near letter quality), and draft quality. The better the printout needs to be, the more dots per inch the printer must use. Of course, higher-quality printing reduces printer speed.

Fonts

All characters of a particular typeface—that is, all the uppercase and lowercase letters, numbers, and special characters—together form a single font. The fonts used for most of the text in this book are Times Italic and Times Roman.

Adding fonts

There are many, many fonts available. Most printers can only handle a few, but some printers allow you to add many additional fonts and enhance your creative freedom by means of soft fonts on removable media, and font cartridges. These are offered by printer manufacturers and third-party font publishers; you must buy them separately.

Typeface Width

On most printers, you can also set the width of the character set, measured in characters per inch (cpi). Proportional-width fonts are also widely offered; with proportional fonts, each character takes space in proportion to its inherent size. For example, a lowercase *l* occupies half a space, and a lowercase *m* occupies a space and a half.

Printing Speed

Internal printer memory

The time needed for a printer to print a line or page not only varies from printer to printer, but also depends on what is being printed and how much internal memory the printer has.

Printing speed is usually given in characters per second (cps), or in pages per minute (ppm). Both specifications are deceptive. The specification of cps is not standardized. Often, the carriage return and paper handling times are not included, making the cps rate unrealistic. Be careful of ppm specifications, too. As a rule, the specified number of pages per minute can only be achieved when the same page is printed repeatedly, but not when a similar number of different successive pages is printed.

Buffer Memory

Every printer has some *buffer memory*. This memory temporarily stores print commands coming from the PC until the commands are executed. This is necessary because the PC can transmit data much faster to the printer than the printer can actually print.

Once the buffer memory is full, the PC must wait upon the printer, and is effectively locked until the buffer is free again. This clearly demonstrates the importance of the size of buffer memory. The more demanding your printer requirements are, the more buffer memory you need. Printer memory can be less than 16K if you are using an inexpensive printer for listings and checklists. Sophisticated graphics printers commonly require several megabytes of memory. Remember to ask how, and by how much, you can expand the memory of the printer you buy.

If you need more buffer memory than what your printer provides, there are several options. You can purchase an external printer buffer unit that has additional memory for storing large files. This unit may also be configurable to let more than one PC access the printer at the same time. Another solution is a software application that lets you configure part of your system memory as a printer buffer. These applications are usually packaged with memory expansion cards.

Drivers

Drivers are programs that establish communication between the CPU and its peripheral equipment, such as the printer. Among other things, the printer driver contains a table specifying what information must be sent to the printer for it to initiate a specific action, such as underlining a word or performing a form-feed. Printer drivers are a very sensitive topic. The software implementation (driver) is only partially standardized, because every manufacturer usually specifies different values.

Software manufacturers usually provide printer drivers needed for applications such as word processing programs, so that the application can print its documents. Because of the variety of printers on the market, a limited selection of printer drivers is usually shipped with an application. The printer manufacturer is responsible for providing driver programs for the software you intend to use.

Printer Types

Printers are generally classified according to the method they use for printing.

Daisy-Wheel Printers

A *daisy-wheel* printer is, in principle, a typewriter without a keyboard. The characters reside on the spokes of a wheel, which is located in front of the print ribbon and the paper. The wheel rotates until the needed letter is in place, and then this letter strikes the ribbon and the paper. To get different type widths or a different font, you have to change the daisy wheel.

The output from such a printer is very crisp, but these printers are technically unsophisticated. They are very loud and slow compared to newer devices, and they cannot produce graphics. Daisy-wheel printers are rarely used today.

Dot-Matrix Printers

Dot-matrix printers use dots to print individual characters. These dots are arranged in a rectangle, known as the *matrix*. A particular set of dots is printed for each character. The more dots available in the matrix, the crisper the printed letter will appear. Dot-matrix printers can print graphics.

Pin Printers

A *pin printer* has from 9 to 24 individual pins in the *print head*, which is located in front of the ribbon and the paper. Whenever a dot in the matrix of a character is to be printed, the pins hit the ribbon and the paper.

Because 9-pin printers do not have high enough resolution and do not offer a substantial price advantage, they are now obsolete. On the other hand, 24-pin printers have become very popular. Not only can they print in resolutions up to letter quality, they also offer a broad selection of type widths and type attributes (boldface, italic, underline, and so on). They may even provide a variety of downloadable fonts. In contrast to other types of printers, pin printers readily use fan-fold paper, and can also accommodate single sheets using semi- or fully automatic single-sheet feeders. They can print multiple copies. Their printing speed is considerably greater than that of daisy-wheel printers.

24-pin printers are popular

Be aware that among 24-pin printers, there are tremendous differences in performance. And don't overlook the noise they can make. (You can reduce this with a noise-protection hood.) Some pin printers can print in colors, but the results are usually not very satisfactory.

To avoid buying a pin printer with few printer drivers, make sure that it emulates either the IBM Proprinter XL, the Epson LQ, or NEC P60. Almost every software program on the market has a printer driver for these printers.

For home use, 24-pin printers are completely satisfactory. In the office environment, they are useful when multipart forms are to be printed, if the requirements for quality are not very high, and adequate measures are taken to control printing noise.

Ink-Jet Printers

An ink-jet printer uses fine ink nozzles to print the individual dots, rather than pins. The dots are "sprayed" on the paper from the ink nozzles. Dots immediately next to one another flow together, making the printed image crisper. The performance capabilities of ink-jet printers correspond to those of pin printers. Current models can print up to 300 dpi. However, ink-jet printers are not designed for printing on fan-fold paper or multipart forms, and they operate considerably slower.

Ink-jet printers are quieter

Because the ink-jet printing method is not an impact printing method, you cannot print multipart forms. On the other hand, you scarcely hear anything while this type of printer is doing its fast work. (Its fan, however, may produce some annoying noise.) Some ink-jet printers can produce satisfactory color images.

Printer drivers can be a problem for ink-jet printers, too. Be sure that any ink-jet printer you consider is able to emulate the HP DeskJet or the IBM Proprinter XL.

Black-and-white printers of this type are priced midrange (at this writing, $300 and up). They are particularly useful for printing word processed documents and business graphics.

Laser Printers

High quality and speed

Laser printers operate like photocopiers. After the PC has transmitted the commands for printing a complete page to the laser printer, the page is fully printed in one step. The capabilities of laser printers far exceed those of the other printers described here. Many more fonts are available, and these machines can print attractive charts, as well as handle color printing, with high quality and speed.

The variety of type styles, sizes, and fonts is determined by the *page description language* that the computer uses to communicate with the laser printer. The most widely used are the Hewlett Packard (HP) PCL4 and PCL5, and Adobe PostScript languages. PCL4 is primarily found in low-cost products that use HP emulation. PCL5 is the successor to PCL4 and is considerably more powerful. Be aware that not all HP emulations are the same.

PostScript is the page description language of choice for users with more demanding printing requirements. PostScript laser printers already contain this language when you purchase them. For a fee, PostScript-capable laser printers can be upgraded to PostScript. To print an entire page of text/graphics, PostScript printers require more than 1Mb of printer memory. This accommodates the larger file size, and avoids interference with the PC's operations. Make sure that you will be able to upgrade the printer memory to at least 2Mb.

A laser printer can print many pages in succession, automatically, because the paper in a laser printer is fed from a paper tray. Paper trays that hold up to 200 sheets are available. These printers cannot work with fan-fold paper. Many laser printers need additional equipment to print envelopes, address labels, small paper sizes, or thicker paper stock.

Laser printers are comparatively quiet. The paper transport mechanism does produce some noise. Also, the printing process releases small quantities of ozone. Consequently, you should not put a laser printer immediately next to your work area. If you use the printer continually, make sure the room's air circulation is good.

If you do a lot of printing that requires high quality, a laser printer is certainly appropriate, and worth the relatively high price (at this writing, $850 and up).

Interfaces

Sales literature uses the term *interfaces* to describe the connectors that connect the printer to the PC. Pin printers usually have a parallel interface. Ink-jet and laser printers have both a serial and a parallel interface. Many laser printers now have an AppleTalk interface, allowing you to also connect these printers to Macintosh computers. Macs are very popular in the graphics world.

Printer Expenses

You'll need to be aware of costs on several levels when you shop for a printer.

Hardware, Memory, and Fonts

Many printers that appear to be inexpensive at first eventually turn out to be highway robbery. An affordable, basic printing system may become completely inadequate. After spending time and money on expansions and additional equipment, you may wish you'd purchased the pricier state-of-the-art model in the first place.

When you shop, note the number of supplied fonts, as well as what type widths (8, 10, or 12 cpi, proportional, and so on) and type styles (such as boldface, italic, and underline) the printer can support. Also ask about memory expansion potential and the cost of such expansions.

The size of the printer buffer (memory), its possible expansion, and the corresponding cost are also important determinants. The larger the printer buffer, the quicker the PC can return to other tasks. Requirements depend on printer type. The size of the printer buffer for pin printers and ink-jet printers ranges from 8K to 80K, but the lower limit for laser printers is 512K. A lot more memory may be required for laser printers, depending upon the intended use. See the section on Buffer Memory earlier in this chapter.

For a printer that uses fan-fold paper, find out whether it has a semi- or fully automatic single-sheet feeder. For ink-jet and laser printers, ask about the size of the supplied paper tray and the cost of a larger paper tray.

Supplies

The cost of printing supplies can reverse many a purchase decision. For example, all printers work with standard paper, or the less expensive recycled paper. Some printers require expensive special paper.

The laser unit in laser printers may need replacement according to the Mean Time Between Failure (MTBF) rate in the printer's manual. The average laser engine is rated at 100,000 pages MTBF.

Also think about the cost and per-unit page output of ribbons, or toner or ink cartridges. For the sake of the environment as well as your pocketbook, ask whether you can recycle used ribbons, toner cartridges, empty ink cartridges, and the old laser unit. Many ribbons can be re-inked, and toner and ink cartridges can be refilled.

Maintenance

Printers, especially expensive laser printers, require regular maintenance. Printer parts must be cleaned, and replaced at specified intervals or as needed. Research these costs before deciding what to purchase.

Operation Considerations

Before you buy a printer, you should try it out at the dealer's location. (If you have a laptop computer, doing a trial run is easy.) Do a trial printout using the highest-quality type and some graphics. You need to assess the printing quality, as well as get an idea of the noise produced by the printer.

Printer operation should not be too complicated. On many printers, the power on/off button is difficult to reach. You also may find it difficult to reach and operate the control panel buttons without twisting and turning.

Look for simple operation

Changing the printer ribbon, or toner or ink cartridge, should not result in blackened fingers and clothing. Changing paper should also be relatively easy; it should not require two people. For fan-fold printers, a paper-feed control is useful for tearing off the paper. On laser printers and ink-jet printers, the printed pages should land in a catch bin and not on the floor. Insist on a demonstration.

Instruction Manual

Getting a well documented manual with your printer—that is, one with clear writing and a lot of illustrations—is critical. If this could be taken for granted, we would not mention it here. Unfortunately, this is not the case. Page through the manual and scan a few sections. If the language is stilted or, worse, complete gibberish, you are likely to have difficulty operating the printer. Be sure to examine the documentation before you buy the printer.

Guarantee and Repair Service

The warranty period on your printer tells you what the manufacturer thinks about the product. A six-month warranty is prescribed by law; many manufacturers give a longer one.

Repairs will always take a long time if your dealer does not have an on-site repair facility and must send the device to the manufacturer or a service center for repair. When you make your purchase, get in writing the maximum time for a repair. Find out if there is a local parts supplier or repair center.

It is also important to know what happens if you need repairs after the warranty has run out. Can you still depend on your dealer?

Price

Even when you have selected a particular printer, don't buy it without checking out prices. You can usually do much better than the list price; sale prices (or "street prices") 30 percent below list are common. Unfortunately, there is only one way to find these prices: Inquire at various dealers and mail-order houses, and test the market.

Chapter 10

Input Devices

The most widely used input device for personal computers is the keyboard. And with the introduction of graphical user interfaces such as Windows and OS/2, the mouse is growing in popularity. Other input devices, such as scanners, are also gaining acceptance.

Keyboards

The first PCs were equipped with keyboards known as PC/XT keyboards. In addition to the main block of keys containing letters, numbers, and common typewriter characters, these keyboards also had ten *function keys* on the left, labeled F1 to F10. To the right of the main keyboard was a numeric keypad, as on a calculator, for quick number entry.

The next generation of PCs was equipped with an AT keyboard. It differed from earlier keyboards by having two additional function keys, other special keys, and a different arrangement in the main keypad. The AT keyboard is the current standard.

The keyboards in use today generally have four distinct areas, and 101 keys. You can see this in Figure 10.1. The main keypad takes up the largest portion of the keyboard. As always, this keypad is similar to a typewriter. Above the main keypad, you will find a row of ten or twelve function keys, numbered from F1 to F12. The Esc key may be in this row, too. To the right of the function keys are six more command keys. At the right end of the keyboard are the cursor-control keys numeric keypad.

When you shop for keyboards, pay attention to the click noise—the sound that occurs when you depress the keys of the keyboard. Though it is frequently claimed that click noise helps you recognize more quickly when you have depressed a key far enough for it to send its message to the computer, you may find the clicks annoying and might want to look for a quieter keyboard. Another characteristic to pay attention to is the keys' resistance to pressure.

Figure 10.1: An extended keyboard

You'll have to try out a keyboard for yourself to decide whether it is the right one. Take your time, and type in a small amount of text on various keyboards; choose the one that feels "right." Make sure that you have at least two choices for the slant of the keyboard. Your wrists will thank you for setting it at just the right tilt.

Mice

Mice were invented to increase "user friendliness." They became very popular with Windows and OS/2. You use a mouse to guide a small cursor (an arrow or some other symbol) on the screen. With this cursor, or *pointer,* you not only can choose menu items quickly and easily, but also select and manipulate text and objects, draw, and design. You click (press) the buttons on the mouse to send commands to the computer. The mouse is often used in concert with the keyboard.

In addition to the most widely used mouse that has two buttons, a three-button mouse is available. Three-button mice are used mostly by application programs that are specifically programmed to use the third button. As a rule, you can switch between using a two-button and three-button mouse without any compatibility problems. The third button simply has no effect when the application is not programmed to use it.

To increase freedom of mouse movement, some manufacturers eliminated the cable connecting the computer to the mouse. The computer receives motion data from these mice by radio or infrared light. One disadvantage of these mice is that they need their own power supply, usually a battery.

When choosing a mouse, make sure that it fits comfortably in your hand and that your wrist is almost straight when you're operating the mouse (see Figure 10.2). You must be able to control the mouse arrow over the entire screen by moving the mouse with your wrist resting comfortably on your work area. To accommodate left-handed people, the software for many mice lets you switch the device to left-handed movement. The mouse should have as high a resolution, that is, accuracy in its signals, as possible.

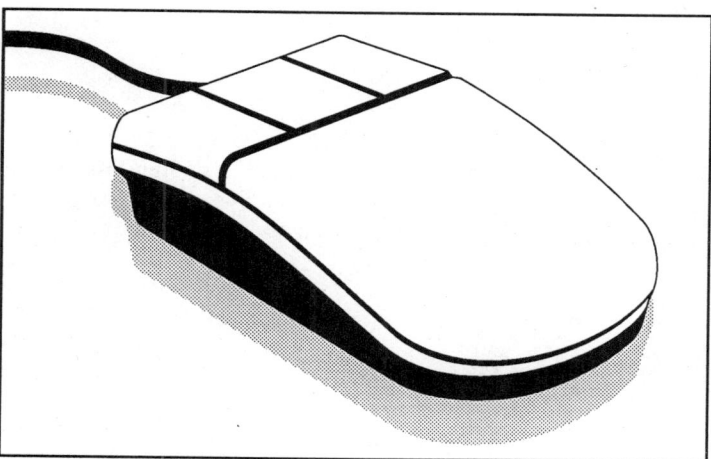

Figure 10.2: Try out a mouse to make sure it fits easily in your hand

Serial or Bus Mouse?

Once you have decided to buy a mouse, you have another selection to make. Should the mouse be operated by way of the computer's serial port or directly over the AT bus? With a serial interface, the mouse only has a plug on a long cord. You must have an open connector or serial port on your PC for this mouse plug. An AT bus mouse is connected to an add-in card inserted into an expansion slot of your computer, so you don't have to use up a port. Generally, bus mice are more expensive because you also have to pay for the add-in card.

When purchasing a mouse, make sure that it comes with the correct mouse driver to act as a translator between the mouse and the computer. Otherwise, the mouse won't work.

Other Input Devices

Though the mouse and the keyboard are the two input devices you will use for most work, some other input devices are used by specific programs.

Joysticks

Playing games on the PC

In the PC arena, *joysticks* of various types are used mainly for games. This is the most entertaining way of spending time with a computer. A PC usually has a connection called a *game port*, where you connect the joystick. If you want to buy a joystick, make sure that it is an analog device; these are the only type that you can connect to your PC. Digital joysticks are intended for home computers other than IBM and Macintosh, such as Amiga, Atari ST, Commodore C64, and Apple IIgs. Joysticks can only be connected to a PC via a special add-in card.

Trackballs

A *trackball* is an upside-down mouse. Instead of moving the mouse case to move a ball underneath, with a trackball you use your fingers to rotate a ball about its own axes within a case. Just as with a mouse, this moves a pointer on the screen. Working for long periods of time with a trackball is more tiring than working with a mouse.

Graphics Tablets

Graphics or *digitizing tablets* (see Figure 10.3) are used primarily in CAD applications (computer-aided design). A tablet uses a mouse with cross hairs or a light pen. You can do the same work with these devices as with a mouse. Usually, you will find menu items as illustrations on the tablet rather than the screen. You can select these items directly using the cross hairs or the pen. These input devices

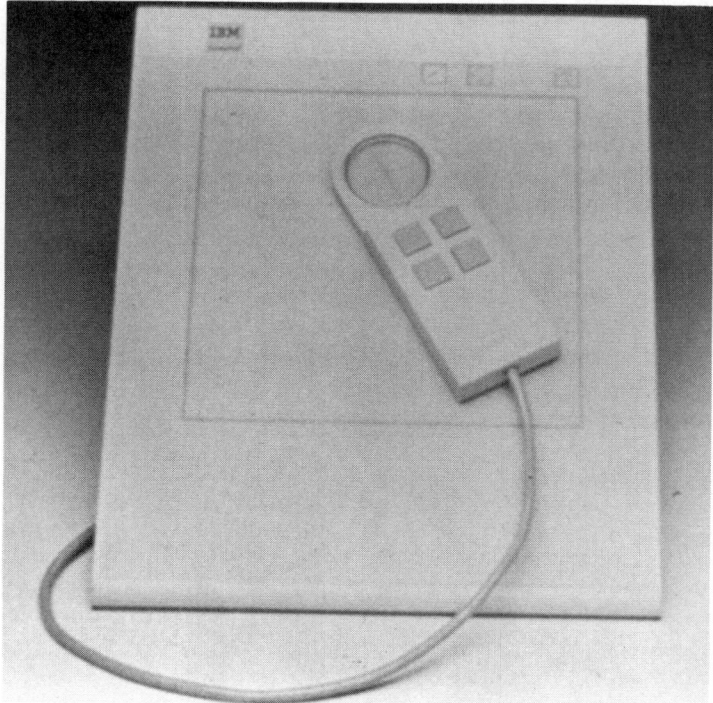

Figure 10.3: Graphics or digitizing tablets are used primarily in CAD applications. Photo courtesy of International Business Machines Corporation.

are used in the professional drafting and design fields, usually with very expensive programs.

Scanners

If you want to teach your computer to read, get a *scanner* with Optical Character Recognition (OCR) software. With a scanner, you can read graphics into your computer and then work with them.

There are also programs that recognize scanned text (for example, a newspaper article) and allow you to store it as a text file. You can search stored text for keywords. Other capabilities you can explore with a scanner are image processing and editing.

Scanners teach the PC to read

The selection criteria for scanners are similar to those for printers. Resolution is the be-all-and-end-all of scanner selection. Measured in dpi, the scanner resolution specifies how many dots per inch the device can read into the computer—the greater the resolution, the better the results achieved. With single-color scanners, it is important to know what color of light is used by the scanner, because that color on the original copy is lost in the scanning process.

Scanners are classified as flat-bed or hand-held scanners, depending on the type of operation. With a flat-bed scanner, you can read 8½ × 11 originals in one pass. Just like a photocopier, you place the original under a cover and let the scanner do the rest.

Hand-held scanners must read larger originals in pieces, for example, the left side of a letter-size page and then the right side. Once both parts are scanned into the computer, you can put them together again using special programs. When scanning by hand, you must manually guide the device, which is like a mouse, over the original. If you move the device around in uneven motions while scanning, or vary the speed of the scan too much, the reproduction in the computer becomes distorted. However, using the supplied software, you can usually correct these errors.

Chapter 11

Other Hardware Options

So far in this book, you have become acquainted with the most important components of a PC system. However, there are still many hardware options that you can use to tailor your PC system exactly to your needs. We have selected a few devices from the variety that is currently available, and describe them here with their potential uses.

Modems

A *modem* (MOdulator/DEModulator) is used to turn acoustical signals (sound) into digital signals and then back again to sound. With a modem, you can easily connect your PC to a telephone line.

A modem connects you to the telephone system

A major technical difference between modems is the speed at which they transmit data (symbols per second). This transmission rate is measured in *baud*. At this time, 300, 1200, 2400, and 9600 are the most common baud rates. When selecting a modem, choose one that has a baud rate at least as fast as the baud rate of the modems you will "talk" to most of the time. Faster modems usually can adjust to slower transmission rates of other devices.

When selecting the baud rate for the modem you buy, consider both your telephone bill and the charges of the on-line services you plan to use. If you send 1Mb files at 1200 baud versus 2400 baud, or large files over long distance using hookup services such as Tymnet or Telenet, the added expense of the faster modem is quickly absorbed by lower on-line and telephone costs. And other services, such as on-line database services, have their own fees and charges.

Of course, the modem hardware alone is not enough; you will also need a program to operate the modem. Commercial programs such as SmartCom II, CrossTalk XVI, and Mirror III are available from your dealer or a mail-order source. Also, there are some *shareware* programs available. These programs, such as Telix, Telemate, and Red Ryder, are available from on-line services, bulletin boards, user groups, and electronic hobby shops. Shareware programs can be freely copied. Once you pay a registration fee, you receive instructions and other services and become a registered user.

Bar Code Readers

With appropriate software, you can use bar code readers to interpret the patterns of vertical lines you see on almost every product you buy in grocery, department, and other retail stores. By reading the code, the computer recognizes the product and can find the price set for it. These devices are primarily used at the cash register computers in large department stores, and for taking inventory.

Plotters

Plotters are special printing devices for graphics output, and excel in line drawing. There are various technologies available. As you may gather from the name, these devices work with pens. The plotter does not draw a series of individual dots. Rather, the PC tells the plotter the starting and the ending points of the line. The plotter puts the pen at the starting point and draws a continuous line to the end point. Plotters can have several pens, so various colors and line thicknesses are possible.

These output devices are mainly used in graphic drafting and design. Because larger drawings are needed in this area, up to 36 inches wide, there are also appropriately large plotters. The price for such a pen plotter can range from $800 up. You can even get plotter-type units for cutting out vinyl signs, such as those used in window displays. Other plotters use thermal, laser, and electrostatic technologies. Plotters like these cost in the $3,000 to $15,000 range—not exactly ideal for home use!

Sound Boards

There are two main uses for *sound boards*, which cost about $125 and up. You can use a sound board as a MIDI (Musical Instrument Digital Interface) and connect your PC to a musical keyboard. Then, using your computer, you can mix several musical parts and accompany yourself while playing the keyboard.

Probably the most frequent use for sound boards today is for computer games, but they are used in many other applications, as well. For instance, you can connect your PC to your stereo system by way of the sound card, and then enjoy almost all your games in great stereo sound. You no longer have to put up with that squeaky integrated PC speaker! Sound boards are becoming more affordable, and are used in applications such as Windows, educational software, and multimedia.

Video Digitizers

Would you like to see how your partner looks with a beard, freckles, pimples, or a hooked nose? Would you like to do other, more meaningful work in the area of image processing? If so, a *video digitizer* could be just the right device for you.

In contrast to a scanner that you use to enter photographs, drawings, and text into a computer, a video digitizer lets you process video signals. You can connect a video recorder, video camera, or camcorder to your PC, record a picture with your PC, and then edit it, store it, install it in programs, or print it out. Incidentally, the T-shirts, calendars, pillows, and so forth bearing portraits and other complex drawings that you see everywhere are created with the help of a video digitizer. Many state motor vehicle regulation agencies use this technology to record your picture on your driver's license and in the agency's database.

Emulation Cards

You can turn your PC into a computer terminal with the help of an *emulation card*, This gives you access to the world of mainframe computers. By way of data transmission or a direct connection, you can work directly on the mainframe computer of your company or of a university. Common emulations are IBM 3270 and DEC VT100.

Much More Hardware Is Available

Of course, there is a wide variety of other possible hardware extensions for your PC. Do you want to control your burglar alarm by computer? Would you like to use your PC to water your flowers? You will find helpful suggestions for projects like these at your dealer's store or in PC-related magazines and other publications. Rest assured that, somewhere, there is just the right solution for your PC needs.

Chapter 12

Operating Systems

The operating system of a computer is the interface between applications programs and the computer hardware. It is a group of system programs that make the computer hardware operate, and make it possible for you to get your work done. The programs within the operating system interpret inputs, display characters on the screen, exchange data with the disk drives, and perform many other basic tasks. Without an operating system, almost nothing can work on your PC.

MS-DOS

MS-DOS stands for Microsoft Disk Operating System. This is the standard today for PC operating systems; even the first PCs were equipped with this system. MS-DOS was supplied by Microsoft as a so-called OEM (original equipment manufacturer) product to manufacturers of IBM-compatible PCs. In those machines, DOS was often customized to the particular characteristics of the computer, if necessary, and then sold with that computer only.

The current standard: MS-DOS 5.0

Frequently, the terms DOS or MS-DOS represent both MS-DOS and PC-DOS (IBM). In the world of PC vendors and users, this is no problem. PC-DOS differentiates the DOS packaged with IBM machines from the DOS used by compatibles.

Although MS-DOS has undergone constant development, it continues to be based on the standard set by the first PC. This ensures that older programs will operate on a PC with newer versions of the operating system. However, MS-DOS cannot make full use of the performance potential of the 80286 processor used in AT computers since 1984.

DOS has been available in version 5.0 since the autumn of 1991. This version contains substantial improvements over its predecessors. For example, version 5.0's memory management is considerably more efficient than that of version 4. When buying a new PC with MS-DOS, make sure that you get version 5 or later.

MS-DOS is a single-user/single-task operating system. This means only one user can work with one program on one computer. Thus, if you want to format a new floppy disk and write a letter, you must do these activities one at a time. Although the disk formatting runs automatically and without your having to do anything after you start it, you must wait until that task is finished before starting another one, such as writing a letter.

Scarce Memory

Limits for
programs
under
MS-DOS

Under MS-DOS, you have a maximum of 640K of working memory. Normally, the operating system and the device drivers also reside in this memory area. (These drivers are special programs for controlling additional hardware, such as a mouse or special video or printer setups.) The memory available for applications under MS-DOS 5 is therefore reduced to about 600K.

In computers with an 80386SX or better processor, it is possible to move the device drivers and parts of the operating system into other areas of memory. This way, more than 600K of memory may be freed up for applications to use. This counting of bytes may seem like small potatoes to you, but even a few kilobytes of additional memory can decisively simplify and accelerate execution of a program.

Graphical User Interface

The
DOS Shell

MS-DOS 5.0 comes equipped with a *graphical user interface* (GUI, pronounced "goo-ey"), the DOS Shell (Figure 12.1). This interface helps the user with everyday tasks such as starting a program or formatting a floppy disk. Instead of typing in complicated command sequences, you can easily select and start the desired task or function with the mouse, by just pointing to the item on the screen and clicking the mouse button.

The DOS Shell also provides an overview of the contents of your hard disk and floppy disk at any time. Several programs can be started at once from the interface. Only one program runs at a time; the others are suspended.

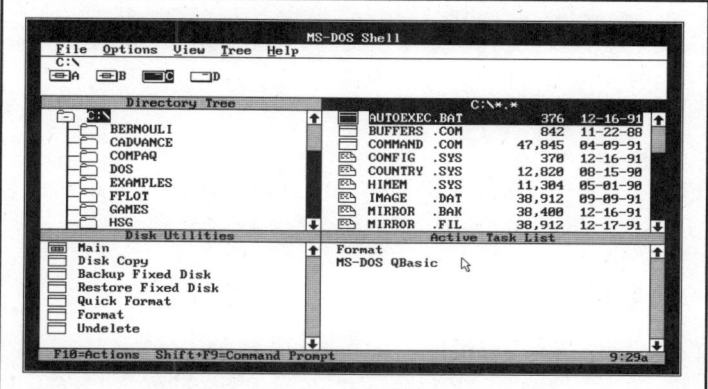

Figure 12.1: The MS-DOS 5.0 DOS Shell

The design of the DOS Shell generally follows the IBM standard CUA (Common User Access). This is based on the idea of designing all programs so that they can be operated in the same or similar ways. For example, saving a file and exiting the programs would be done by clicking or entering the same commands. The CUA rules have pretty well established themselves in the world of PCs, and most new programs follow them.

CUA

DOS 5.0 Accessories

If you find you cannot get used to a graphical user interface, you can still enter your commands at the DOS command line. To help you in this, you can employ a *command-line editor*. This editor stores the command lines you enter and keeps them ready for later use, so you don't have to reenter the same or similar commands from scratch. Instead, you can simply call them up, modify them, and execute them.

DOS 5.0 offers *help text* for every command. This help text provides information on the parameters and options permitted with the command.

Just like the first DOS versions, MS-DOS 5.0 also contains a *BASIC interpreter.* It is called QBASIC and is compatible with the popular Microsoft Quick BASIC. Beginning programmers will find it helpful.

An elementary *text editor* is available with the DOS command EDIT. This is a special call to the QBASIC editor that you can use to edit plain text.

DR DOS 6

Intended compatibility with DOS 5.0

For several years, Digital Research Inc. has offered its PC operating system, DR DOS (Figure 12.2), as an alternative to MS-DOS. The various versions of DR DOS are meant to be compatible with MS-DOS. All programs that run under MS-DOS should also run under DR DOS. At the same time, DR DOS always has several improvements over the current MS-DOS version.

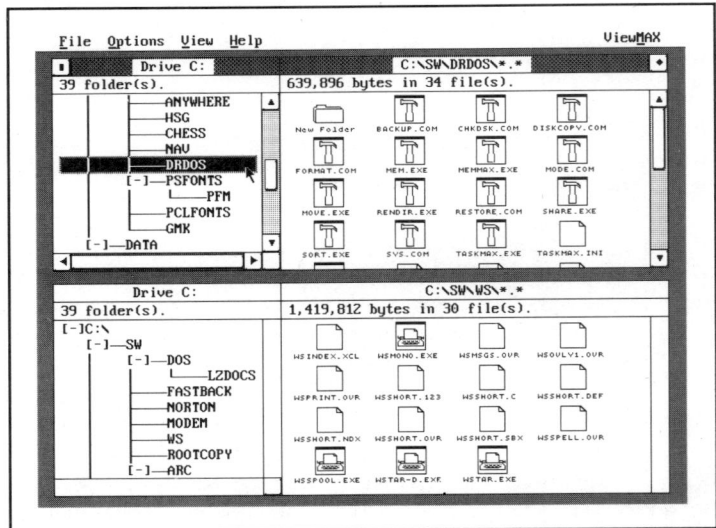

Figure 12.2: The Viewmax user interface in DR DOS 6.0

Earlier versions of DR DOS were not completely compatible with MS-DOS. There were occasionally problems with programs that ran easily under MS-DOS. These problems have been somewhat alleviated with version 6.0, but there are still some compatibility glitches, especially with Windows 3.1.

When comparing DR DOS 6.0 to MS-DOS 5.0, another disadvantage of DR DOS is that it does not contain a BASIC interpreter. If you are not interested in BASIC, this should make no difference. Other users, however, will have to invest additional money for a separate BASIC interpreter.

Against these disadvantages stand several advantages. DR DOS 6.0 places more available working memory (a maximum of about 627K) at the disposal of your applications. It also provides better hard disk management. Programs and data may be compressed before storing, allowing the hard disk to hold almost twice as much data. In addition, data transmission is faster, although the time gained during transmission is offset by the time needed for compressing data during storing and decompressing the data during loading.

More memory and higher disk capacity

Data transmission can be improved even more using the high-speed *disk cache* program supplied with DR DOS 6.0. Additional utility programs are available to reorganize a hard disk so that even more time can be saved when loading programs and data.

Fast disk cache

Under DR DOS 6.0, individual files and directories can be made secure with *access protection*. This way, if a PC is used by several people, the work areas of various users can be reliably separated. This protects against intentional mischief and unintentional destruction.

Access protection

Finally, DR DOS 6.0 costs less than MS-DOS 5.0. However, don't be distracted by the version numbers; DR DOS's higher version number is more of a marketing ploy than an indication of advanced development. In all other areas, these two competitors are very similar. The decision is up to you.

Windows

Microsoft Windows is an extension to the DOS operating system and cannot run without DOS. It is a graphical user interface whose features extend far beyond those of the DOS Shell. Several million copies of Windows version 3.0 have been sold, and version 3.1 is just as popular.

Microsoft first released Windows in 1984. The goal of this graphical user interface is to make the computer friendlier to you, the user. With Windows you do not need to learn the "language" of the computer. Applications and related files are presented as symbols (*icons*) on the screen. To start a command, you simply press a key or click the mouse.

The appearance of Windows version 3.0 corresponds to a large extent to the CUA standard. Windows 3.0 will run on all PCs, including those with an 8088 or 8086 processor, but you need a faster processor for truly effective computing. With Windows 3.1, you need an 80286 processor at the very least.

Conventional DOS programs run under Windows either in windows on the screen (in 386-enhanced mode) or as full-screen applications. Programs developed especially for Windows retain their normal appearance, but make full use of the Windows graphics capabilities, as well. Owing to the market success of Windows, nearly every software developer has started generating Windows-compatible versions of their programs. Also, Windows accessory programs are available to accomplish many tasks within Windows itself, as explained in the next section.

In 386-enhanced mode, Windows also permits *multitasking*, which means several programs can run at once (see Figure 12.3). By the way, the example we used above—formatting a disk and typing a letter—is not true multitasking. It is virtually impossible to work with one program while a floppy disk is being formatted in the background. However, with other combinations of applications, multitasking operates satisfactorily under Windows.

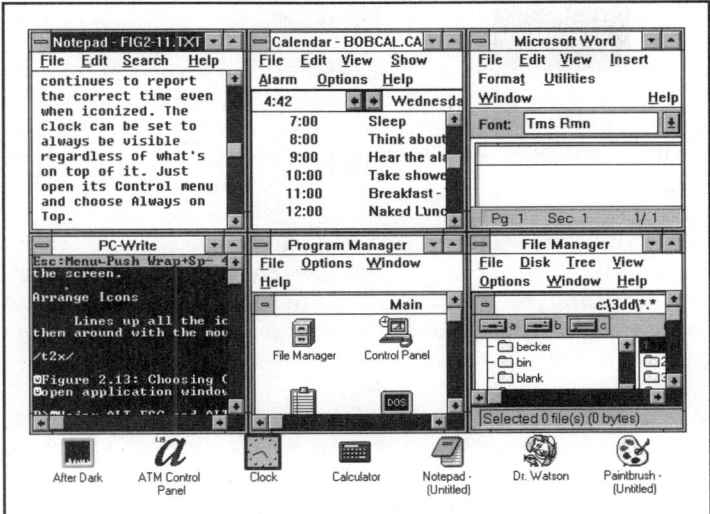

Figure 12.3: Windows 3.1 with several windows active

Though DOS programs each must be tailored to the available hardware, Windows programs are device-independent. You customize Windows once. Then, the programs use what Windows prescribes.

Windows Accessories and Games

As you might expect, the Windows package supplies a wealth of programs. These include, among others, the word processing program called Write, which allows you to generate documents quickly and easily. Paintbrush is a drawing program you can use to produce graphics. Additional accessories are Terminal, for exchanging data with other computers; an on-screen Calculator; an electronic Cardfile; a Clock and a Calendar; and Notepad, a scaled-down version of Write.

You can get a lot of practice operating the mouse while enjoying Solitaire, Reversi, and Minesweeper, three games supplied with Windows. (Reversi is not bundled with Windows version 3.1.)

Games

Choosing an Operating System

MS-DOS continues to be the standard operating system for PCs. The only alternative for computers with an 8088 or 8086 processor is DR DOS. For computers with newer processors, the difference between MS-DOS and DR DOS is relevant only in special circumstances.

With an 80286 or better processor, you should consider supplementing your DOS with Windows. Windows has become very popular, attracting software and hardware developers to design compatible products. Consequently, in the future you will rarely have trouble finding suitable software, even driver programs.

When deciding to buy, consider the hardware you now have. If your PC has an 8088 or 8086 processor, it makes no sense to purchase Windows. It runs as slow as molasses on these computers, and offers almost no advantage over DOS 5. With these computers, you should stick to DOS.

Even with AT-compatible 80286 computers, you should purchase Windows only if some other prerequisites are satisfied: Main memory should be at least 2Mb—4Mb are even better. Because Windows accesses the hard disk often for temporary storage, you need to have a fairly fast disk. Hard disks with an access time exceeding 30 ms are too slow.

You cannot make use of the multitasking properties of Windows unless you have at least an 80386SX processor. Additionally, you need to have 4Mb of main memory and a fast hard disk with more than 40Mb of storage to make working with Windows really fun.

If you are going to buy a computer with these or better equipment features, OS/2 2.0 is an interesting alternative for you. Let's take a look at this option.

OS/2

Microsoft and IBM together developed OS/2 as a successor to DOS. For the first time, an operating system could utilize the potential of the 80286 and newer processors. (Since then, the paths of the two companies appear to have parted. Microsoft concentrated on Windows, and IBM has continued to develop OS/2.)

Earlier OS/2 versions numbered 1.x are geared to the 80286, the typical AT processor. The newer product line, OS/2 2.0, is a true 32-bit operating system that assumes you have at least an 80386SX processor.

OS/2 is a multitasking operating system. It can execute several programs at one time. It also is not limited to the traditional 640K memory limit of MS-DOS. You can directly address 16Mb of real memory. By swapping some program sections to the hard disk, programs can use up to 1 gigabyte. In this way, the narrow limits set by DOS for PC programs are bypassed.

True multitasking

OS/2 2.0 for 80386 processors

OS/2 2.0 solves many of the incompatibility problems experienced by users of the earlier OS/2 1.x versions. This new version of OS/2 has the following characteristics, features, and capabilities:

- A prerequisite for using OS/2 2.0 is a computer with a 32-bit processor, that is, at least an 80386SX with 4Mb of main memory and about 32Mb of space on the hard disk.

- Under OS/2 2.0, you can run DOS, Windows, 16-bit OS/2 programs (these are the programs of OS/2 1.x) and 32-bit applications simultaneously on one computer.

- In theory, with version 2.0 you can run up to 240 DOS programs simultaneously (multitasked) in the foreground or background, as full-screen applications or in windows. Every DOS program runs in its own virtual environment and is completely separate from other programs. Yet the programs can still exchange data dynamically.

- The hoarding of memory for DOS programs is less of an issue. Every DOS program can use about 630K of memory. Added to this are up to 32Mb of EMS memory and 16Mb of XMS memory.

- A few older applications require specific DOS versions. Therefore, every DOS environment under OS/2 2.0 can be configured so that it corresponds to the needed DOS version.

Windows programs under OS/2 2.0

OS/2 2.0 was designed to attract Windows users, and Windows-compatible programs can be executed directly from OS/2. This opens the broad market of existing PC programs for the OS/2 user. Also, developers can fully exploit the capabilities of the 32-bit microprocessor. This way, you can use programs with considerably greater performance than ever would have been possible under DOS.

The OS/2 2.0 graphical user interface has also been completely redeveloped and redesigned. It now corresponds to the newest CUA standard. It is now known as the Workplace Shell (Figure 12.4). Though it takes some getting used to for anyone who has previously

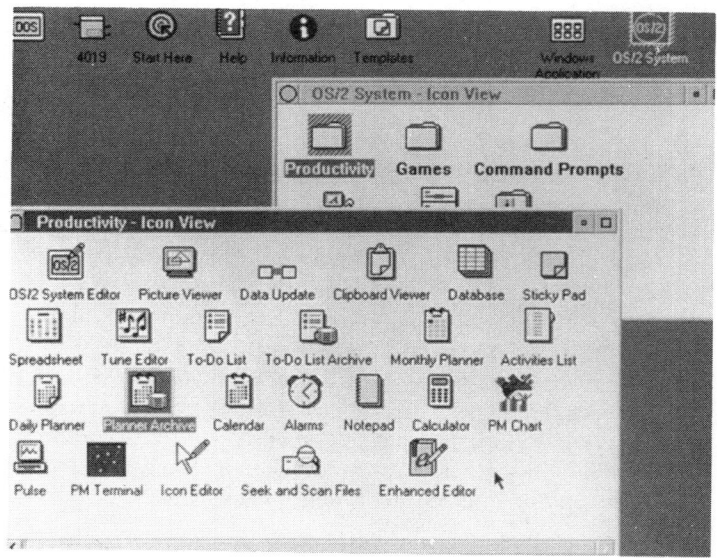

Figure 12.4: The Workplace Shell of OS/2 2.0. Photo courtesy of International Business Machines Corporation.

worked with Windows, simple tasks can still be accomplished immediately, and without a learning curve. You can also call up more detailed information by accessing learning (tutorial) text and reference (help) text.

OS/2 2.0 Accessories

As is customary in graphical operating systems today, OS/2 2.0 also contains several accessory applications. These include the OS/2 system editor, a text editor for generating and editing files, a terminal emulation program, a database program, a graphics program, and about 20 other useful small programs. There is an on-line reference manual. Various games (chess, solitaire, Reversi, and so on) are also supplied.

IBM tested OS/2 2.0 on computers of other manufacturers and published the results. Because of this, many device drivers are supplied.

Device drivers are available

Should You Consider OS/2 2.0?

The minimum hardware requirements listed above can be considered only suggested guidelines. A typical OS/2 2.0 workplace should have at least 8Mb of working memory and a hard disk with considerably more than 40Mb; 80Mb is a suggested minimum allocation. Though almost every PC can be upgraded easily to these standards, remember that, as a 32-bit operating system, OS/2 2.0 needs at least an 80386SX processor. So if you want the option of upgrading to OS/2 2.0, your computer must contain at least this level of processor.

Demanding hardware requirements

Our own tests of OS/2 2.0 have shown that many standard DOS programs run without problems. Some Windows applications were also tested and worked satisfactorily. You should view this information with caution, however, because we could not, of course, test all available programs.

You should expect good support for OS/2 2.0 problems, because of IBM's interest in having this system succeed in the market. In addition, OS/2 2.0 is comparable in price to DOS 5.0.

When you buy an 80386 computer, you are taking a small (financial) risk in buying OS/2 2.0. On the other hand, you will immediately have available several programs, together with the capabilities of a truly advanced operating system. If you choose OS/2, and your computer is not from IBM, you should test before buying to find out whether the computer and OS/2 will work together without problems.

Chapter 13

Software Tools

Computers and their programs are not independent of one another. Every program needs the hardware and the operating system in order to run. Your selection of a PC therefore will depend on the work you want the PC to do. In larger professional workplaces, a very specific set of functions can be allocated for every machine. In the home and in smaller offices, however, the PC must fill many roles. You probably want to be able to deal with a growing flood of data now—with the original equipment you are buying—without having to define each individual task before the purchase. To help you, this chapter describes common types of popular software applications and defines important hardware requirements.

One way to check and test specifications is to read computer magazines and visit appropriate specialty dealers. There, you can get descriptions of various programs and then compare them at your leisure.

Word Processing

Word processing, as its name implies, produces text; it is by far the most widespread PC application. Word processing is very popular because it provides fast and easy error correction, and the potential to format and display text on the screen. There are many word processing applications. They place different demands on the system and, of course, have different costs.

You will have to define your word processing requirements fairly precisely. The basic functions listed below are only a small sample of the many capabilities offered by a modern word processing program.

- Simple corrections of typing errors
- Deleting, copying, and moving blocks of text
- Special text attributes (boldface, italic, and underline)
- Automatic hyphenation

- Inserting automatic line breaks and page breaks
- Production of headers and footers
- Form-letter production
- Grammar checking

Many programs offer a *WYSIWYG* display—this means "what you see is what you get." The program displays text on screen exactly as it will appear later after printing. This saves you from having to print out the text in order to check your formatting.

Especially for beginners, it can be very helpful if the word processor's user interface (as well as that of other programs you use) has been designed according to the CUA (Common User Interface) standard described in Chapter 12. This will make it easier for you to learn the program.

The hardware requirements for today's non-Windows-compatible word processing programs are modest. Usually, a PC XT with 640K main memory, a hard disk, and a monochrome (black-and-white, green, or amber) display is sufficient. As the functionality of a word processing program grows, so do its hardware requirements. For example, if you frequently use grammar checking and hyphenation, a faster processor (80286 or better) and faster hard disk (about 20 ms) can shorten your wait time. A VGA or SVGA video system is easier on the eyes and works better with mouse-driven and Windows-compatible programs.

If you want to produce more than just plain-vanilla letters—reports, text in various typefaces and heights, and graphics, for instance—you should consider programs that run under Windows or OS/2. Such programs (Word for Windows, for example) use the WYSIWYG concept. Of course, these programs have greater hardware requirements. A PC with an 80386 processor, 4Mb main memory, a clock speed of at least 20 MHz, and an appropriately fast hard disk will usually provide adequate response time.

Remember that the printer determines the real and final appearance of your text. Thus your printer purchase is just as important as your choice of PC. Type produced by a 9-pin printer is not letter-quality text. The printer used for high-quality output should be at least a 24-pin printer or, better, an ink-jet or laser printer.

Database Programs

Databases help manage a collection of data that belongs together. A variety of programs that let you generate, manage, and query (get reports from) a database are available for the PC.

At its most basic, a database and its related queries correspond to an electronic index card file. This file might contain the names, addresses, game records, and other data on all members of a chess club. A database provides many advantages over the paper index cards. For example, the database can instantly provide, using an alphabetically sorted address list, a list sorted on dates of birth or the length of club membership.

There are a variety of complete database systems available for general applications such as managing addresses. The example of managing addresses clearly demonstrates that data should be stored in a standardized format. You can then use the data in a word processing program to address form letters.

In PC programs, the database file structure usually follows the standards set by Borland's dBASE program. However, the means for generating and querying databases vary considerably. For example, with a program from Computer Associates, called Clipper, you can devise and compile a stand-alone program around the dBASE standard. In addition, you will find third-party development tools for working with databases. With such tools you can quickly build databases with simple to complex input/output functions.

Databases run on computers of all sizes, from microcomputers up to mainframes. The hardware required for database operation depends on the program. The quantity of data to be managed is also very important. For home use, a PC AT with an 80286 processor is usually adequate if you have plenty of hard-disk space. You should have as much hard disk space as is practical, and the disk should be as fast as you can afford.

Spreadsheet Programs

A *spreadsheet* is ideal when you have extensive calculations to do, or when you must frequently repeat the same calculations using different numbers.

In these programs, the screen is set up as a worksheet divided into rows and columns—electronic ledger paper, as it were. In some fields, you enter the numbers to be used as a basis for the calculations. You enter the equations in other fields. Equations link numbers from the other fields. A field with an equation displays the current result of the equation, not the equation itself. Spreadsheet programs, as a rule, can display their results not only in tabular form but also in graphical form, such as pie charts and bar charts.

Be aware that spreadsheet programs are memory hogs. The more memory your PC has, the better; you should have at least 640K. Also, because of the constant recalculations, we recommend a processor that is as fast as possible—at least an 80286. If you are going to do engineering calculations, a math coprocessor will definitely help.

You will also need a high-resolution printer for these applications, to exploit their graphics capabilities. You'll be able to generate truly professional business presentations in this way.

Desktop Publishing

You will be able to produce your own high-quality publications, in house, with *desktop publishing* (DTP) programs. The tedious procedure of taking copy outside and then correcting it again and again becomes unnecessary with DTP.

Indeed, several PC programs are now available that accomplish this. In professional desktop applications, Macintosh computers from Apple have become dominant. Nearly all the major DTP programs that run on IBM and compatible machines are used with Windows.

Remember that these complex programs are somewhat difficult to learn. If the saying, "Time is money," applies to you, include the cost of training in your purchase decision. It helps to know something about typography, but this isn't required.

The video card, display, and printer used for DTP must all be of high quality to produce satisfactory results. All three devices should provide the greatest resolution possible. Select a monitor that is as large as possible—larger than 14 inches. An absolute necessity for DTP programs is a flicker-free display, with a refresh rate greater than 70 Hz at maximum resolution.

We recommend a fast processor and hard disk because of the complexity of computations necessary in DTP functions. Consider an 80386 with a 33-MHz clock and at least 4Mb RAM. The hard disk should be large—at least 80Mb.

Integrated Packages

A few software publishers offer *integrated software*. These packages combine several applications into a single program package. Well-known examples are Lotus Symphony, Microsoft Works, and WordPerfect Office.

These packages provide advantages to anyone wanting to use several standard applications such as word processing, spreadsheets, and databases. You can easily exchange data between the programs of the integrated package. For example, it is very easy to write a form letter using the word processor and then address it to a group of names stored in the database.

If the integration is well designed, all its programs have a similar user interface and thus operate consistently. This dramatically reduces the learning curve. You can produce quite professional results using the different parts of the program.

When selecting suitable hardware for one of the integrated program packages described here, remember two things. First, the minimum requirements stated by the software publisher must be satisfied. Second, the various program parts make different demands on individual components of the PC. Therefore, be sure that each part of the program operates efficiently on your system. If in doubt, select higher-grade hardware just to be safe.

Business Applications

In addition to the software described above for general office applications, there are many applications for specific business tasks. For example:

- Financial accounting
- Order processing
- Accounts receivable and payable
- Payroll
- Real estate management
- Inventory management

When searching for the business application suitable for your specific business need, it may be difficult to find good advice. Looking in the computer magazines won't help much, because programs such as these are rarely the subject of comparison tests. The best help is available in trade journals. Special publications such as *InfoWorld*, and catalogs from computer expositions and fairs provide an initial overview of available programs. (The premier computer fairs are, of course, the Boston and San Francisco Computer Fairs.) Generally, visiting an exposition will give you the opportunity to personally compare competing products and get advice from competent people at the booths.

In addition to the performance characteristics of these programs, you also should keep a few other important criteria in mind. The program should be either a network version or capable of being upgraded to a network version. If several people are to use the program, multi-user access protection is recommended. Interfaces to other programs of this group are important. This permits, for example, storing addresses only once. Have the dealer demonstrate the interaction of the programs!

A quality software publisher provides support even after the sale. A telephone hotline is very useful for resolving problems as quickly as possible. Free correction of bugs should absolutely be expected. Though all this is true of all high-quality software purchases, it is especially important in a business-specific application. Competent installation help, advice, and employee training can be important during the introduction phase and is the responsibility of the retail vendor.

When selecting hardware required by business applications, get the advice of an experienced user, if possible. Here are some guidelines:

- Do not take the minimum requirements of the software publisher too seriously. On the minimum setup, the program will usually be quite sluggish. If you hire an hourly employee to operate your business's financial accounting program, the additional cost of better (faster) hardware will quickly be absorbed.

- The more data you have to be processed, the faster your computer and hard disk should be. The guiding principle should be how much time is required to process the data. If, for example, you only do accounting for about four hours per week, an 80286 computer and a 40Mb hard disk are sufficient. However, if you employ a full-time accounting assistant, you should have at least an 80386, 20-MHz machine and an 80Mb hard disk with average access time less than 20 ms.

- Don't pinch pennies on the monitor and video card. Both should have flicker-free operation (refresh rate greater than 70 Hz) and a resolution of at least 800 × 600.

Vertical Market Applications

Special programs are available for individual professions. Today you find a computer in just about every doctor's office, for instance. This computer not only maintains the patient list (address management), but also handles billing. Frequently, other processes, such as printing prescriptions, are integrated in the system. Vertical market solutions are available for many occupations. There are systems for the construction trade, for craftspeople, for freight handlers, and for farmers.

The hardware needed in these environments is, accordingly, very system specific. We advise against purchasing such a system "over the counter" and installing it on your own. You will not only have problems setting up the working environment but will also sorely miss needed technical assistance when starting the system and running it.

When selecting the software, keep two things in mind: First, prepare as detailed a set of specifications as possible. You have to recognize all functions—even the most obvious and elementary ones—that the selected program should provide. Nothing is an "obvious" component for such a system. Second, it is very important to visit users who already have the software package installed and have been working with it for some time.

Programming Languages

Programming languages allow you to write down computer instructions in a readable text form. The various languages use their own words and logical constructions to do this. The program source code must then be translated into a form understandable by the computer (machine language).

There are two different methods of implementing such a translation: the compiler and the interpreter.

Inter-preters

An *interpreter* is a program that reads through the program code line by line. Every line is translated into machine language and executed immediately. This makes developing a new program very quick and simple to do. Every line of program code can be executed, checked, and corrected, if necessary, immediately after you enter it.

However, there are a few disadvantages to this technique. Because the interpreter must translate the entire program every time you run it, it executes slowly. You can't execute the program without the interpreter.

A *compiler*, on the other hand, completely translates the program code and then produces machine-readable code. This process is supplemented by another program, known as a *linker*, before the executable program is produced.

Compiled programs can run by themselves and are much quicker than interpreted programs. They do not need to share the available memory with an interpreter and can therefore be larger. The program development is more complicated, however, because you can only test a complete program.

The issue of which language is the best programming language constantly results in heated debates among programmers. We cannot give you a simple recommendation, because every language has advantages and disadvantages. Here are some guidelines:

- The BASIC interpreter, QBASIC, comes bundled with MS-DOS 5.0, so this is a good and easy place to start. BASIC is easy to learn and also surprisingly powerful.

- Among the class of program compilers, Borland's Turbo Pascal has become a virtual standard. Many computer magazines publish programs and routines in this language.

- Professional applications frequently use the C programming language. C compilers were at first only available in programs running under DOS. Windows-based C programs were introduced in 1991. This was also true for OS/2 programs.

- There are many general-use, as well as specialized languages. For example, COBOL is geared to business applications; FORTRAN is geared to scientific applications.

If you want to dig deeper into one of these wide-ranging topics, you will find additional details in related technical journals.

Chapter 14

Communications

In addition to word processing, managing data, and financial accounting, you can use your PC to communicate with other computers or computer systems. For example, using your computer, you can get the latest news directly from press agencies, look at stock quotes on various stock markets around the world, access special on-line databases, or even send a fax. You can also connect to other computers—for example, to your company's main headquarters. Data from the order-taking department can be communicated directly to the warehouse. The purchasing department can call up stock inventories directly from the warehouse computer.

Data Transmission

The term *data transmission* covers almost everything involving computers and the transmission of data. In the general area of data transmission, there is a whole range of additional services and possibilities that you might find interesting, as described in the following paragraphs.

On-Line Databases and Information Systems

Knowledge is power; this is just as true today as it has ever been. Today you can dial into data services with a modem and call up data. There are many different on-line databases. For example, there are services for lawyers that store important verdicts, in addition to text and comments on legislation. Using a search criterion such as "computer crime," you can transfer *(download)* information about this subject into your home or office computer and evaluate it later. In addition to such special information systems, there are also more general database systems.

The largest on-line service in the world is CompuServe. You can dial this service from almost anywhere in the world. Of course, there are other services available—America Online and GEnie are two well known examples. However, you might want to initially become acquainted with the on-line world by studying and using CompuServe. The major areas of information provided by CompuServe are categorized as described here:

- *Business Management and Reference:* In this section you will find information on various occupational interests (medicine, journalism, computers, and so on). You can get conference dates, statistics, survey results, and much more.

- *Electronic Mail (e-mail):* Here you can send and receive messages to other users; join an on-line computer conference with participants from around the world; and read and post advertisements. You can also send public opinion letters to legislators.

- *Computers and Technology:* This is the largest part of the system. You will find information about different types of computers and can contact the manufacturer if you have questions. User groups and special interest groups (SIGs) have their own areas *(forums)*. Many companies use these forums to gather information concerning their newest developments, and to get user perspectives. Of course, articles from the major computer magazines are available for reading, hot off the press. You will also find comprehensive offers for interesting software and shareware. Publishers and developers answer questions and give tips and tricks. You will also find valuable contacts to user groups in your vicinity.

- *Education and Reference:* In this area, you can start studying, take tests, find specialized knowledge, read dictionaries, look at teaching information, and so forth.

- *Entertainment and Games:* Here you will find reviews and reports on games, and tips and tricks for playing. You also can make contact with publishers and developers to talk about your problems and ideas. There are also many games that you can download to your computer and enjoy off line.

- *Money Matters and Markets:* Here you will find everything about money: banking information and broker tips; statistics from the last 12 years; market analyses and sales growth rates of various companies; and expert projections. Whether you are looking for innovations in banking, information on consulting firms, or statistics in specific investment areas—if you cannot find it here, it probably doesn't exist.

- *News, Weather, and Sports:* All the information available in newspapers is readily available on line. It makes no difference whether you are looking for general information, whether you take a special interest in sports, or prefer to look at the financial information from Reuters. Everything is available here, just waiting for you to access it.

- *Shopping Services:* You can buy just about anything you want, from a new car to flowers, from accessories to toys, from books to facial cream, all on line.

- *Home, Health, and Family:* This section covers a wide range of topics about your health, pets and equipment for them, astrology, comics, music, religion, cooking, and much more. You will surely find information about your hobby here. You might even find someone local with the same interests.

- *Travel Services:* Are you taking a trip and want to quickly book a flight or a hotel? Do you need a rental car or information about the weather? Do you need to clarify something with your credit-card company or get tourist information on a particular country or city? You will find your answers in this area of the CompuServe system.

As you might expect, CompuServe is a commercial enterprise, just like most other on-line database and information systems. This means that you must pay to use the system. Usually, you pay a monthly fee plus charges for time on the system. You can get basic services for a flat $7.95 per month at this writing. For more detailed information on the charges and current features of a system, check directly with the company. You can usually find addresses and phone numbers in computer magazines.

Fax by PC

External and internal

You can buy either an external fax component or a fax board that plugs into a slot on your motherboard. PC fax add-ons usually also have an integrated modem. These options are as easy to work with as a simple modem and can perform most functions of a fax machine. What's different from the conventional fax machine is that with a PC fax, you send and receive the text or graphics directly via the computer (rather than writing or printing it first). Thus, you cannot send handwritten notes or other hardcopy.

To receive a fax, your computer has to be on line at the time. The information received is either printed out immediately on your printer or stored on a hard disk or floppy disk. If your computer is in your bedroom, we recommend the second choice.

Be aware that PC fax add-ons may be receive-only, or send-and-receive units. Most fax modems come bundled with the required software.

Intracompany Communication

To make companywide computer communication possible, the computers must be "wired" together. This requires special add-in cards and appropriate software. Once wired together, the computers are available as a computer *network*. Because of the complexity of network concepts, the different network types are not described in this book.

With the right software, you can send reports from any computer to any other computer on a network. You can also fetch data from any computer to any other. Data can be protected by a password. There are a great many possibilities available, starting with sending simple memos and reports, to automatic communications between computers. If, for example, the address of a customer is updated on one computer, this new address becomes available immediately to all users of the network. For instance, you might have purchase orders prepared automatically by the computer in a purchasing department using data available on a computer in the warehouse.

As you can imagine, the potential of networked computers within a company is tremendous. If such a network connection is of interest to you, contact a specialized dealer and get advice in more detail about how to convert your tasks to a computer network. The cost is not cheap. Take your time.

Chapter 15

Choosing Software

You can't do anything with a computer by itself. It is the software, the programs, that make a computer live. In Chapter 13 you learned what types of programs are available, such as word processing and file management. In addition to deciding what software to buy, you need to decide how much money you want to spend. There are also different sales paths. This chapter throws a little light on these subjects.

Retail Sources for Software

Programs in this category are at the upper end of the price spectrum. As a rule, you also get some other benefits for your money. Only dealers who have been selected for their technical knowledge and training may sell these products. At least, that is the publisher's intent.

In addition to specialized technical advice, you also get support from a knowledgeable dealer as long as you use the product. The dealer will help with most problems and questions, and will refer you to the publisher only in really difficult cases. Ask about this. If this service is not provided, you may want to choose another dealer.

Specialized technical advice

After registering the product, you will be kept up to date by notices from the publisher regarding innovations. If a new version of the program appears, you can usually buy an updated version at a reduced price. Frequently, the manufacturers of these programs also provide a hotline—a telephone number from which registered users can usually get their questions answered and problems solved for free. Check out these hotlines before deciding. Some are over-loaded, and you frequently get only a busy signal when you call. And then, when you do get through, you get a recording saying, "...Our office is closed now. Please call during office hours..."

Authorized dealers will frequently offer training (that you must pay for) in the use of some products. Again, ask about this before purchasing.

Programs sold by authorized dealers need to be first class not only in service and support. Their high price should also come with a high standard of operation and performance features. You can find out about this only by a thorough demonstration. In some price ranges, you should be able to visit a user who has had the product installed for some time. If the dealer has no time for you, move on.

Of course, it does not make economic sense to buy a word processing program from an authorized specialty dealer if all you want to do is write plain, everyday correspondence. On the other hand, if you want to work with complicated products such as DTP or CAD, the authorized specialty dealer is the best purchasing source.

Software manufacturers do not always require qualification of dealers. Accordingly, you will often get no advice when purchasing. The salespeople may not know the answers to questions. In these situations, the sale is the only goal.

Before buying a program with unregulated distribution, you should thoroughly research the product yourself. Possible sources of information are technical journals, the software makers themselves (who will usually provide free lists of features), and independent testing institutes. The Software Publishers Association (SPA) sets standards for software produced by its members and creates a forum for interaction between publishers and users.

In addition to having the functions you want, it is particularly important that there be a service center for the product, for example, a telephone hotline from which you can seek support for problems. Many publishers provide this telephone customer support. Employees are available during business hours, sitting at a computer, ready to answer your questions and help solve your problems. Because use of customer support lines is often restricted to paying customers, rather than owners of pirated copies, you usually need to send in the registration postcard accompanying your program. Also, you may be asked for your registration number when you call. But even if you forgot to send in your card, try the support line anyway.

Public Domain Software (PD)

It is hard to believe, but true. There are free (almost) programs! You can get *public domain* (PD) software at various PD mail-order houses for a small copying fee (about $3 to $5). These programs are also available for downloading from on-line services, and sometimes included on companion disks in books.

"Free" software

There are two different types of PD software. There are complete programs that dedicated programmers generously release to the public *(freeware)*. Some authors, as well as publishers of commercial programs, release free demonstration versions of their programs *(demos)*, to stimulate the purchase of a complete version. The demos usually have some key features disabled.

The complete PD programs are usually not as full-featured as their more expensive commercial versions, but they do their job. Now and again, you will find a PD software jewel that is every bit as good as commercial software. At such low prices, it is well worth the effort to look at three or four PD programs for personal use. You can then use one or all of them. For professional use, PD software is probably not the best choice, although demos may help in decision making.

Shareware

Shareware is a mixture of commercial and PD software. Just like PD programs, you can obtain shareware for a small registration fee (or sometimes just a postcard to the author!). Meanwhile, many department stores, computer shops, and bookstores are selling shareware. For a modest charge, you will get a small manual and the program.

These shareware programs are sometimes limited versions of another software package. By making another small payment directly to the shareware author (you will find the address on the disk), you can obtain a complete version with a full manual. Publishers of shareware also often provide support, such as a hotline.

Limited features

Complete features, but limited use

Some fully functional shareware programs give you permission to use the program for evaluation purposes for a few days, or a certain number of saves or executions. After this limit is reached, permission expires and the program stops functioning. Once you pay a license fee directly to the shareware author, you receive the right to unlimited use and frequently get full documentation and access to customer support.

Pay those shareware fees!

The shareware author trusts your honesty. If the program continues to work even when the time period has passed, don't exploit this fact. The license fee is usually small compared to the price of commercially sold software; however, the programming effort to create these tools is often the same. When shareware fees aren't paid, authors stop writing these often valuable programs as shareware, and turn to commercial avenues instead.

The Importance of Comparable Interfaces

An important consideration when purchasing PC software is that user interfaces, that is, the appearance and the operation of the software, are not standardized. The need for a standardized user interface among applications has led to the establishment of the Common User Access (CUA) interface, a set of terms, keystrokes, and commands created by IBM. Still, every publisher is, for the most part, working without compliance standards.

In the absence of standards, try to buy programs with comparable interfaces.

One method of keeping training expenses as low as possible is to buy programs from a single company. Or you can buy programs intended to be regularly used together—for example, a word processing, drawing, and database program—from the same publisher.

Where to Buy Software?

You should check out a few current computer magazines to gather information about a given program before buying it. There are even special-interest magazines dealing only with freeware and shareware.

Ask your dealer. And consult the forums of on-line services, too.

When selecting software, first consider where and to what extent you are going to use a program. Sometimes public domain or shareware products suffice for private use. For businesses, you will want a commercial product, so that when problems do occur, your work won't be interrupted for too long. It is, of course, a great advantage if a knowledgeable dealer is there to help immediately. However, the software manufacturer is ultimately responsible for supporting its own product.

With a little luck, you will find complete comparison tests for the programs you need. When searching for these in computer magazines, a telephone call to the publisher may lead to the appropriate issue. Computer magazines also carry advertisements. You can then request a list of features from the publishers.

A few publishing houses have produced market overviews for software programs. You can obtain these in most major bookstores. Look for *PC Magazine*, *PC World*, and *InfoWorld*. In these, you will find short descriptions of the software, the vendor's address, and prices, all classified by type of application.

You also will find comprehensive literature on almost every PC program in the Computer or Business sections of bookstores. There are many books available to help you choose and learn to use just the right program for your needs.

Once you have selected software, ask about it at several dealers. There are considerable price differences, up to 50 percent in extreme cases. If you cannot expect help from a dealer in your vicinity, but the software manufacturer provides customer service, do not be afraid of ordering from a mail-order house. Prices are often lower at these sources, as well. You will find their addresses in computer magazines.

Chapter 16

Choosing Hardware

Just as for software, there are several paths you can take in buying hardware. With hardware, there are only two different types to consider: no-name (generic) and brand-name equipment.

Equipment Differences

The most obvious difference between generic hardware and brand-name equipment is the price. But before you quickly check the generic product on your shopping list, consider the other differences—they involve more than just having a brand name on a metal plate.

Service

You should always keep customer service in mind when shopping for hardware, just as you do for software. Don't expect to place high demands on the service provided by the small-time operators who assemble computers from many inexpensive parts and then sell them in a small local store, or by the well-known discount chains using their own names on the equipment.

Advice

You will immediately know if salespeople are really advising you or just passing the time of day. Whether you are in a computer store, a jewelry store, or a clothing boutique, if you are about to spend a large amount of money, you should expect competent advice.

Uness you've done your homework, you are easy pickings for many a salesperson, especially those working on commission. If you enter a store with technical knowledge gathered beforehand, however, and an idea of the equipment you want for your system, you will often receive considerably more polite and technically competent advice.

If you are offered a computer that *almost* corresponds to your needs and requires only small changes, tell the dealer. It will not be difficult for the dealer to convert or install multiple floppy drives, add a hard disk drive, a different video card, more memory, or just about anything else. In the end, the customer is always right. Your wishes are important.

Repairs

The chapters of this book that talk about various pieces of hardware also discuss the problems that may occur. If it is not just your hard disk or some other independent part that is defective, one that can be repaired simply by exchanging it or removing and fixing it, your entire computer unit will have to be given to a repair technician. If the technician does not work locally, your unit must then be shipped to another site, where it sits in a completely overloaded workshop until someone gets around to looking at it.

On the other hand, if you have purchased brand-name hardware from an *authorized* dealer, you can usually assume that an on-site technician is employed. (Ask to make sure.) If the defect cannot be quickly fixed without a long wait, you will often receive a replacement unit for use during the repair period. Occasionally, you are asked to pay some rent on the loaner.

So if you want to avoid having to wait six weeks for your computer to be repaired, ask about repair facilities and procedures when buying. Get promises of expected repair time in writing.

Warranty Period and Guarantee

The warranty period is a simple indication of the quality of a device, and of the manufacturer's general confidence in the device. Knowledgeable users expect a warranty period of at least six months. Some generic products and brand-name hardware are sold with a warranty period of up to three years. In particular, well-known computer chains with branch offices tend to give longer warranty periods. Their manufacturers simply replace defective units.

Another indication of the quality of generic hardware is whether the dealer offers an extended warranty on the equipment, in addition to the manufacturer's.

Compatibility of Individual Components

As you have already learned in the preceding chapters of this book, the individual components of a computer must work together. The necessity of successful interaction is particularly important in the video system; however, you should make sure that all other components also work properly together. For example, if you are offered a "standard system" with 8Mb RAM and a 20Mb hard disk, or if you are offered a cache memory as an accelerator with a 28-ms hard disk, you should know to ignore these offers. Look for contradictions in the capabilities of the equipment.

Environmental Protection

Almost all the components of a computer, and its hardware and software expansions, will eventually wind up in a hazardous materials disposal site—after years of loyal service, of course. Various metals and chemicals would be released if this equipment were placed in a simple landfill, thereby posing risks of poisoning ground water and air. Think about this when making your purchase!

A few computer manufacturers, primarily IBM, offer recycling programs for their customers. For a few components, this environmental protection program pays for itself. Precious metals such as gold, silver, and platinum were built in during the manufacture of these devices. Recycling takes two forms: actual recovery of the precious metals, and reuse of consumables. A large market exists today for refilled laser toner cartridges and reinked printer ribbons.

Consider, also, the quantities of packaging material involved in storing and transporting a computer or almost any expansion device. Find out if you can send your packaging material back to the dealer, who may be able to reuse or sell it. Before disposing of packaging material, think whether you will need it again for moving or shipment. Some manufacturers only honor their warranty, according to the warranty conditions, if the device is sent back in the original packaging. Ask your dealer about this.

Chapter 17

Sample Systems

This chapter describes possible sample systems for typical work areas with a PC. Obviously, these examples can only serve as ideas and not as a standard solution. These are minimum solutions that will allow you to work effectively.

Office Workplace

Nearly every office today has a PC. It should be an IBM-compatible PC with at least an 80386SX processor, a 40Mb hard disk with less than 30 ms access time, one 5.25-inch high-density floppy disk drive, a standard VGA video card, and a low-emission color monitor with a refresh rate of 70 Hz (flicker-free). With this system, you can write letters, manage a database, do spreadsheet calculations, and generate business graphics. By adding 2Mb RAM, the Windows graphical user interface program can be used on this system.

An ink-jet or laser printer will provide quiet efficiency. However, there can be problems with a laser printer if labels or envelopes are to be printed. If this computer must generate documents with copies, the computer probably should also have a dot-matrix printer. Often, several computers within an office share one printer. The connection between each computer and the printer must be established using some sort of switch.

For software, this workplace needs a word processing program, a database management program, and a spreadsheet program with integrated graphics functions.

The New Office

In new offices, such as the one in Figure 17.1, and those looking toward the future, you will find computers with one of the graphical user interfaces: Windows or OS/2. With these systems, user convenience is enhanced by graphical symbols and icons for specific commands. Many programs run similarly on these interfaces, by

Figure 17.1: The PC in an office. Photo courtesy of International Business Machines Corporation.

means of mouse clicks, standardized menus, keyboard shortcuts, control menus, and shared temporary storage (a Clipboard). When you buy new software for the computer, you will only need a fraction of the previous learning time, and time is money!

The IBM-compatible PC in this environment will have an 80386 processor with a clock speed of more than 20 MHz. It will have at least 4Mb RAM on the motherboard. In addition to a hard disk with about 80Mb of storage capacity and an average access time of less than 20 ms, there also will be a 3.5-inch HD floppy disk drive and a 5.25-inch HD floppy disk drive, typically in a tower case. To make effective use of the graphical capabilities of this system, a SuperVGA card and a low-emission color monitor, both with a resolution of 800×600 dots and a refresh rate of at least 70 Hz, are necessary. A mouse is just as important for this computer as the keyboard. You also will need a printer and software corresponding to your production needs.

DTP and Graphics

For graphics and DTP, you will need a very fast computer, to create and display your layouts and graphics quickly. For this, you will need an IBM-compatible PC with an 80386 processor having a clock speed of 33 MHz or faster. It also should have a large hard disk (120Mb) with an average access time considerably less than 20 ms. A working memory of 4Mb RAM is necessary; 16Mb is recommended.

You should have a SuperVGA video card and a 16-inch color monitor, at least, connected to this computer. The video card and monitor should have resolutions of up to 1024 × 768 dots and a refresh rate of at least 70 Hz. To be ready for anything, you will need both 3.5-inch and 5.25-inch HD floppy disk drives. Such a computer should have both a keyboard and a mouse.

Under certain circumstances, you may also need a scanner to import original graphics. You will also need a laser printer for satisfactory results.

CAD

To satisfy computer performance expectations in a PC workplace doing CAD work, you really need an IBM-compatible PC with an 80386 processor and an 80387 math coprocessor, or an 80486 processor. Figure 17.2 shows an example of a CAD workstation. To avoid frequent accesses to the (relatively) slow hard disk, as many operations as possible should be done in the memory of the computer. Therefore, plan on from 8 to 32Mb RAM for this unit. To have enough space for your finished calculations and designs, you will need at least a 120Mb hard disk with an average access time of less than 20 ms.

A Super VGA video card with a resolution of 1024 × 768 dots is recommended, so that your designs do not look like they were built with children's blocks. An eye-saving, high-resolution, at least 17-inch color monitor with 1024 × 768 resolution and a refresh rate greater than 70 Hz (noninterlaced) will make your work easier. In addition to a mouse, you will need a digitizing tablet for your input. As output devices, you will need a dot-matrix printer for test outputs and a pen plotter for later production drawings. You will of course need a CAD program on your hard disk.

Games

You can play games with almost any PC. However, to enjoy most of the new games, you will need a few extensions to your computer. Of course, you should have a VGA video card and a color display. You can control most games with the mouse, many even with the keyboard. However, for most games, we recommend you purchase a joystick. Consider buying a sound card to improve on the monotone sound that comes from the built-in speaker. Moreover, with this

Figure 17.2: A computer for more demanding work: a CAD workstation. Photo courtesy of International Business Machines Corporation.

sound card you can connect your computer to a stereo system and enjoy music and synthesized sound of high quality. If your favorite games are flight simulators and the like, you should have a PC with a heavy-duty fast processor, for example, an 80386.

Chapter 18

Hardware Checklists

The foregoing 17 chapters have given you the most important information you will need to purchase a PC. So that you don't overlook anything during the purchase process, study and use the following checklists.

The PC

Product:		
Manufacturer:		
Processor		
Clock speed in MHz		
Wait states		
Coprocessor with same clock included?		
Socket for coprocessor included?		
Main memory/RAM in Mb		
Maximum Mb RAM expandable on board		
Cache memory in K		
Serial ports		
Parallel ports		
Game port		
8-bit slots		
16-bit slots		
32-bit slots		
5.25-inch drive slots (HD or DD)		
3.5-inch drive slots (HD or DD)		

Case type		
Keyboard type		
Clear documentation?		
Warranty period		
Duration of a repair		
Replacement unit during repair?		
BIOS (type and date)		
BIOS update available?		
Price:		

Hard Disk Drive

Product:		
Manufacturer:		
Entered in BIOS setup under which name?		
Controller type		
Capacity in Mb		
Heads		
Cylinders		
Average access time		
Interleave factor		
Installation frame necessary?		
Installation height		
Noise level		
Warranty period		

Immediate exchange for defects?		
Clear documentation?		
Price:		

Floppy Disk Drive

Product:		
Manufacturer:		
5.25-inch, 360K		
5.25-inch, 1.2 Mb		
3.5-inch, 720K		
3.5-inch, 1.44Mb		
Installation frame necessary?		
Noise level		
Ejection mechanism		
Warranty period		
Immediate exchange for defects?		
Price:		

Printer

Product:		
Manufacturer:		
Printing principle		
Number of pens/jets		
Resolution in dpi		
LQ printing speed		

Draft printing speed		
Fan-fold paper		
Single-sheet format		
Prints labels?		
Prints envelopes?		
Number of character sets		
Serial interface		
Parallel interface		
LocalTalk and other interfaces?		
Automatic interface switching?		
Friction feed/tractor feed		
Semiautomatic single-sheet feed		
Fully automatic single-sheet feed		
Printer buffer in K		
Emulations		
Font cartridges		
PostScript capable?		
Automatic emulation switching?		
Printing noise		
Cost for ribbons/ink/toner		
Recycling available?		
Cost for special paper		
Cost of accessories (paper bins, cut sheets feeders, cables)		
Printer driver		

Repair duration		
Warranty periods		
Price:		

Mouse

Product:		
Manufacturer:		
Serial interface		
Bus mouse		
Resolution in dpi		
2 or 3 buttons?		
Handy shape?		
Mouse driver?		
Clear documentation?		
Warranty period		
Replacement or repair for defects		
Price:		

Video Card

Manufacturer:		
Type (VGA, etc.)		
Maximum resolution, noninterlaced		
Refresh rate at max. res., noninterlaced		
Colors at max. res., noninterlaced		
Memory in K		

Graphics chips manufacturer?		
Clear documentation?		
Warranty period		
Replacement or repair for defects		
Price:		

Monitor

Manufacturer:		
Type (VGA, etc.)		
Screen diagonal measurement		
Maximum resolution, noninterlaced		
Dot pitch		
Analog or digital input		
Monochrome or color		
Fixed-frequency or multifrequency		
Refresh rate at max. res.		
Matches video card?		
Demonstration date		
High contrast		
True colors		
Sharp contours (check s, a, and e)		
Antiglare housing		
Monitor base available		
Low emissions? Ergonomic?		
Warranty period		

Repair or exchange for defects		
Repair duration if applicable		
Clear documentation?		
Price:		

Chapter 19

Software Checklists

Preparing a software checklist is difficult, because varying criteria are always involved in choosing a software package. There are many hundreds of applications for the PC. So, we first give you a few general items to check. The checklists themselves should be viewed more as guides than complete lists of specifications.

General Questions to Ask

1. Get a list of features from your dealer or directly from the software publisher. Prepare a list of minimum functions that you must have in the program. How do they compare?

2. For which operating system is the program written? Is this a single- or multi-user (network) program?

3. What are the *minimum* hardware requirements for operating the program? What is the recommended setup for *satisfactory* operation? For *better* operation?

4. With what other programs can the program exchange data (e.g., database management and word processing for form letters; graphics creation and a spreadsheet for business graphics)?

5. Does the publisher regularly update the program? Is the program undergoing further development? When did the last version come out? Has a newer version already been announced? Are free, automatic updates provided if an update is expected soon after your purchase?

6. Is the documentation adequate?

7. What printer drivers are supplied? Who will help if the program does not have needed drivers for printers, video cards, or other peripherals? What will it cost?

8. What support services are provided (hotline, new version updates, regular written information)? At what cost? Can

you call the hotline now to see if it's always busy? Is there an 800 number?

9. *Ask questions!* Don't be shy about asking the meaning of unknown words or technical content. You don't have to be an expert in technical jargon.

Word Processing

Product:		
Publisher:		
Operation:		
Menu control		
Command control		
Mouse support?		
Interface: DOS, Windows, or OS/2?		
Character Features:		
Number of character sets		
Variable character size		
Italic		
Boldface		
Underline		
Subscript/superscript		
Block/Paragraph Functions:		
Tabs		
Indent		
Variable line spacing		
Cut, Copy, Paste		

Document Functions:		
Variable page size		
Variable print area		
Macro programming		
Macro recorder		
Text modules		
Headers/footers		
Page numbering		
Form letters		
Columns		
Additional functions:		
Hyphenation		
Grammar checking		
Thesaurus		
Tutorial		
Basic calculations		
Lines/boxes/tables		
Inserting date		
Automatic backup		
Printing Functions:		
Your printer supported?		
Adjustable print quality		
Queue		
Abort/restart		

Import/Export of Files:		
System files		
ASCII files		
Other word processing programs		
Database programs		
Spreadsheet programs		
Graphics programs .		
Modem:		
Price:		

Database

Product:		
Publisher:		
Prerequisites:		
Minimum RAM		
Minimum hard disk in Mb		
DOS, Windows, or OS/2?		
Operations:		
Mouse support?		
EMS support?		
DOS, Windows, or OS/2?		
Command input		
Control center		
Additional Features:		
Tutorial		
On-line help		

Editing/programming		
Report generator		
Label output		
List output		
Form-letter functions		
Relational data linking		
Graphic data evaluation		
Address managing		
Text editor		
Runtime module		
Program generator		
Mask generator		
Application Language:		
Macro		
SQL		
QBE		
C		
dBASE		
BASIC		
Specifications:		
Number of commands		
Number of data types		
Number of records		
Number of fields per mask		
Number of users (with code)		

Export/Import of Files:		
ASCII		
dBASE		
Lotus		
Excel		
Paradox		
Word processing programs		
Other		
Add-in Modules:		
Calendar		
Calculator		
File manager		
Spreadsheet		
Price:		

Product:		
Publisher:		
Prerequisites/Operation:		
Minimum RAM		
Minimum hard disk in Mb		
DOS, Windows, or OS/2?		
Coprocessor support		
Mouse		
EMS support		
On-line help		

Specifications:		
Max. number of columns		
Maximum number of rows		
Max. row size		
Max. users		
Number of math equation functions		
Number of simultaneous worksheets		
Additional Features:		
Worksheets in 3-D		
Macro language		
Business graphics module		
Database functions		
Word processing		
Calculator		
Import/Export of Files:		
ASCII		
dBASE		
FoxPro		
Lotus 1-2-3		
QuattroPro		
Excel		
Other		
Price:		

Chapter 20

Glossary

640 × 80, 1024 × 768, and so on: Specification of the maximum resolution of a video card or monitor.

8086, 8088, 80286, 80386, 80386SX, 80386DX, 80486SX, 80486DX, i486: Processor type designations, listed in order of increasing performance. The names i486, 80486SX, and 80486DX are different designations for the same generation processor.

8087, 80287, 80387, 80487SX: Designations for math coprocessors that perform computing tasks for the CPU in programs that support a coprocessor. This speeds up program execution. Coprocessors also come in SX and DX versions (except the 80487SX). Processor and coprocessor must be of the same generation (such as 80386 with an 80387).

Add-in card: An exchangeable computer component.

Analog input: Advanced video cards, such as VGA, transmit analog signals to the monitor. Older video cards transmit digital signals.

Architecture: The technological design of the system bus and the central processing modules.

AT: Advanced Technology. Model name for a second-generation IBM PC. Also used today as a type name for all IBM-compatible clones having an 80286 processor.

Average access time: The time that passes, on average, from when the read/write heads of a hard disk have found data on the disk to when these data reach the processor.

Baby case: A PC case with a small footprint.

Baud: One bit per second (usually). Specification of the transmission speed of a modem.

BIOS: Basic Input/Output System. A program that is always resident in the PC. Allows the various components of the computer to work together. The BIOS is always provided in a configured PC. A PC will not function without a BIOS.

Bit: Binary digit. The smallest data storage unit in a computer. Used to represent numbers and program instructions. A bit can either be set (1) or not set (0).

Byte: Eight bits form one byte.

Cache: Fast temporary storage used in two ways: to accelerate hard-disk access and to accelerate main-memory access by the CPU.

CAD: Computer-aided design.

Central processing unit: Also known as the processor, or CPU. The actual computer that performs the calculations, it is an Integrated circuit made of silicon.

CGA: Color Graphics Adapter. Obsolete video card standard for the PC.

Clock speed: The number of clock cycles of a device, per unit time. The clock rate of the CPU is measured in MHz, thus in millions of clock cycles per second.

Compatibility: Computers and their components are said to be compatible if they may be used in place of (interchanged with) the original components, and the software continues running without problems. An IBM-compatible computer is a generic "clone" of an IBM machine.

Compiler: Utility program that translates human-readable instructions into a midlevel object file which is then linked into a machine-language program.

Controller: Add-in card that handles data exchange between the CPU and the floppy and hard disk drives.

Coprocessor: Additional processor chip that performs special tasks for the CPU. The best known examples are math coprocessors, and graphics processors on intelligent video cards.

CPU: Central processing unit.

CUA: Common User Access. IBM's original design and recommended standard for structuring a user interface.

Daisy-wheel printer: This printer is constructed and works like a typewriter. The letters, positioned just above the paper, strike a ribbon and print the letters on the paper.

Database: Program for collecting and managing related data.

Data bus: The collection of internal lines used for data transmission.

Data transmission: Umbrella term for all types of remote communication among several computers.

DD: Double-density. Formatting method specifying the amount of data a floppy disk can store. DD now signifies a relatively small quantity of data. *See also* HD.

Deflection frequency, horizontal: *See* line frequency.

Deflection frequency, vertical: *See* refresh rate.

Desktop: Describes the GUI-style interface used by Windows, OS/2, and some DOS applications. Also describes the most popular case design of a PC, which sits on top of your desk. *See also* DTP and GUI.

DOS: *See* DR DOS or MS-DOS.

Dot-matrix printer: Characters are composed of dots from a printhead matrix. Every dot of the matrix is produced by a pin in the print head or by an ink jet.

Dot pitch: Spacing of the pixels in the shadow mask of the videomonitor screen. The smaller the pitch, the finer the image.

DPI: Dots per inch. Measurement of resolution of input and output devices.

DR DOS: Digital Research Disk Operating System, an operating system for personal computers. As of February 1992, the current version number is 6. A competitor of MS-DOS.

Driver program: A program for controlling a special peripheral device. Especially for nonstandardized peripherals, communication between the PC and the peripheral can only take place with a supplied driver program.

DTP: Desktop publishing, the technical term for typesetting and layout work using a computer.

DX: Identification for fully functional processors (such as 80386DX), in contrast to SX.

EGA: Enhanced Graphics Adapter. Obsolete graphics standard for PCs with a digital signal output.

EISA: Enhanced ISA. Expanded ISA bus for 32-bit PCs. *See also* system bus.

EMS: Expanded Memory Specification. Method for reconfiguring memory above one megabyte.

Enhanced AT keyboard: The current standard keyboard for PCs, with 102 keys.

ESDI: Hard disk design with high memory capacity, high data-transfer rate, and high price.

Floppy disk: Round magnetized disk (nicknamed "floppy") contained in a rigid or flexible plastic sleeve. Used to store backup copies of programs and data, and to provide a means of installing programs and exchanging data between computers.

Floppy disk drive: Device installed in a PC to read and write floppy disks.

Format: To prepare a floppy or hard disk for accepting data.

Full-duplex: A communications mode that echoes all data received back in the transmitting computer, for example, over a telephone line.

Gbytes: Gigabytes (also abbreviated GB). One Gbyte is 1024 megabytes.

Graphical user interface: An operating environment that runs in graphics mode, letting the user work with applications using mouse clicks on icons and buttons on the screen to select commands and options. Windows and OS/2 are the most popular examples of this type of user interface.

GUI: Graphical user interface. Pronounced "gooey."

Hard disk/hard disk drive: Long-term storage medium for large quantities of programs and data. Hard disk drives contain permanently mounted magnetized disks with read/write heads. The size of the drive is measured in megabytes; the time specified in milliseconds for the drive represents the average access time.

Hardware: Collective term for all physical computer components and peripherals. This includes the computer itself, as well as all attached devices (keyboard, mouse, printer, and so forth).

Hayes-compatible: Established worldwide standard for modem operation, based on modems of the Hayes Company.

HD: High-density. Formatting method specifying the amount of data a floppy disk can store; HD signifies a comparatively large quantity of data. Only floppy disks specified as HD can be reliably formatted for HD. *See also* DD.

Hercules-compatible: Somewhat out-of-date video standard for the PC. *See also* MGA.

Hz: Hertz, the unit specifying how many times a task can be performed in one second. *See also* clock speed and refresh rate.

IDE: Integrated Device Electronics. Advanced type of hard disk controller where controller logic is integrated in the hard disk assembly. It occupies a slot. Fast, reasonably priced. Can usually also control floppy disk drives.

Ink-jet printer: This operates like a pin printer, except that the matrix dots are projected on the paper by an ink jet.

Interlaced: In the interlaced method, when refreshing an image on the monitor, only every second line of the image is refreshed during one pass. This reduces flicker for the entire image, but flicker still appears between two adjacent lines. *See also* noninterlaced.

Interleave: Number of rotations needed by a hard disk drive to completely read one track of the disk.

Interpreter: Program that translates human-readable instructions into machine language, executing the instructions line by line.

ISA: Industry Standard Architecture. The design of the system bus first used in the AT technology.

Joystick: A hand-held control device originally used in video games. In the PC arena, these input devices are used most often in flight simulators or games.

K: Kilobyte, also abbreviated k or KB; 2^{10}=1024 bytes constitute one kilobyte.

Keyboard: Input device with typewriter-style keys, and special function and control keys.

kHz: Kilohertz; 1000 Hertz.

Laptop: Portable PC with built-in batteries providing an independent power supply, usually weighing about 8 to 15 pounds.

Laser printer: Works on the same principle as a photocopier. The image to be printed is exposed on a drum, using a laser. Toner powder is applied to appropriate locations by means of electrostatic charge. By rolling the drum and applying heat, the toner powder is fused to the paper. Laser printers produce images of very high quality.

LIM: *See* EMS.

Line frequency: Specification of how many thousand lines of an image can be redrawn completely per second, expressed in kilohertz (kHz). The line frequency for the monitor and the video card must match. *See also* refresh rate.

LQ: Letter quality; specifies the print quality of a dot-matrix printer.

Main memory: Up to 640K of memory allocated to the CPU. This memory is directly accessible by program instructions and data.

Mb: Megabyte, also abbreviated MB; 2^{10} kilobytes are one megabyte (about one million bytes).

MCA: Micro Channel Architecture.

MDA: Monochrome Display Adapter, an obsolete video card standard for the PC.

MGA: Monochrome Graphics Adapter. *See also* Hercules. Somewhat out-of-date video standard for the PC.

MHz: Megahertz; one million Hertz.

Micro channel: Bus system for the IBM PC. *See also* system bus.

Microprocessor: Semiconductor module with the essential processing unit of a computer.

Modem: Modulator/demodulator. A device for transmitting data over the telephone line from computer to computer

Motherboard: Main system circuit board of the PC.

Mouse: Input device primarily for graphical user interfaces. A ball is located on the underside of the mouse case. This ball rolls when the mouse is moved and transmits motion data to the computer. You make selections by pressing (clicking) two or three buttons on the top.

ms: Millisecond. For hard disk drives, a specification of the average access time.

MS-DOS: Microsoft Disk Operating System. Operating system for personal computers. As of February 1992, the current version is 5. A competitor of DR DOS.

Multitasking: The parallel processing of several programs on a single computer.

Network: At least two computers connected together for communications, data interchange, and shared resources.

NLQ: Near letter quality. Specification of the print quality of some dot-matrix printers.

Noninterlaced: In the noninterlaced method, every line of the image is redrawn on the monitor during each refresh cycle.

Notebook: Portable PC with dimensions about 8½ by 11 inches, about 2 inches thick. It is useful for traveling because of its low weight (about 8 pounds or less) and built-in batteries.

On-board: In PC processors, on-board means that the expansion sockets for main memory are located on the motherboard.

Operating system: The sum total of all system programs that permit operation of the computer hardware. An operating system is required to be able to use applications programs.

OS/2: Operating System/2. Operating system for PCs having an 80286 or better processor. Now developed by IBM as a competitor of Microsoft Windows. Most current version is 2.0.

PC: Personal Computer.

Personal computer: A stand-alone computer available to only one user at a time. Most PC-type computers are modeled after the IBM PC.

Pixel: Picture element (on a video monitor).

Port: A connector for external peripheral equipment, such as a printer.

Program: A collection of commands controlling the behavior of a computer.

Protected mode: CPU operating mode that allows multitasking and improved memory management.

Protocol: In modems, a protocol defines the structure for data exchange between two computers. This specifies how many consecutive *data bits* are used when transmitting information. Depending on the specified protocol, these data bits may be followed by a stop or parity bit.

RAM: Random Access Memory. *See* main memory.

Real mode: CPU operating mode used by DOS.

Refresh frequency: *See* refresh rate.

Refresh rate: Specification of how often the complete image is redrawn on the monitor each second, in hertz (Hz). Refresh rates (noninterlaced) starting at about 70 Hz are flicker free.

Resolution: Specification of how many picture elements can be output by a video card, monitor, or printer. The higher the resolution, the more detailed the image.

RLL: Improvement of the out-of-date MFM method for recording data on a hard disk. Enables higher memory capacity and data transfer rate. Is being superseded by IDE, SCSI, and ESDI.

ROM: Read-Only Memory. Memory area from which data can be read but to which data cannot be written.

Scanner: Hand-held or tabletop device for reading graphics or text into a computer. Using reflected light, the computer receives data in the form of visible dots. With appropriate software, text can be recognized as such, then edited and stored.

SCSI: Small Computer System Interface. Hardware port for up to eight peripherals. In PCs, usually used to connect appropriate hard disks. Permits very fast communication and memory expansion. Latest version is SCSI-2.

Slim-line: Desktop PC with a very thin case.

Slot: Connector for adding in various expansion cards.

Software: A collective term for computer programs.

SuperVGA: VGA cards that, in addition to the standardized VGA modes of operation, also function in higher-resolution modes. These modes of operation are achieved only with an appropriate monitor and video drivers.

SX: Designation for processors with restricted performance, or short instruction set, for example, 80386SX (in contrast to DX, the fully functional version).

System board: Main circuit board of the PC; motherboard.

System bus: The collection of all signal lines in a PC.

Tower case: Design of a PC case. A large, upright (rather than horizontal) unit that has a small footprint and high profile when on the desk, and saves space when off the desk.

Transfer rate: The rate at which data is transferred between the PC and a storage device, measured in megabits per second.

V.21, V.22, V.23, V.24, and so forth: Interfaces defined by the CCITT, for modems and other devices. These specify the standards for communication between the PC and the modem.

VGA: Video Graphics Array. Currently, the most typical standard for PC video cards and monitors. Communication among the PC, video card, and monitor is standardized; VGA also standardizes the maximum resolution, the refresh rate, and the type of signals transmitted (analog). *See also* SuperVGA.

Video adapter: *See* video card.

Video card: A plug-in card (circuit board) that prepares text and graphics for output to the screen.

Wait state: If the components of the PC run at different speeds, the faster component (the processor chip) must wait for the slower one (RAM). The number of clock cycles that pass while some components wait are known as the wait states; "0 wait states" means without wait states.

Word processing program: A program used for creating and editing text, and producing the printed documents.

WYSIWYG: "What You See Is What You Get." A program with this property displays a document on the screen exactly as it will appear when printed.

XMS: Extended Memory Specification. The main memory of a PC above one megabyte.

XT: One of the first IBM PC models. This abbreviation is generally used for all IBM-compatible PCs with 8088 and 8086 processors.

Index